HERE WE ARE, HOME AT LAST

THE ARCHITECTURE OF NITHURST

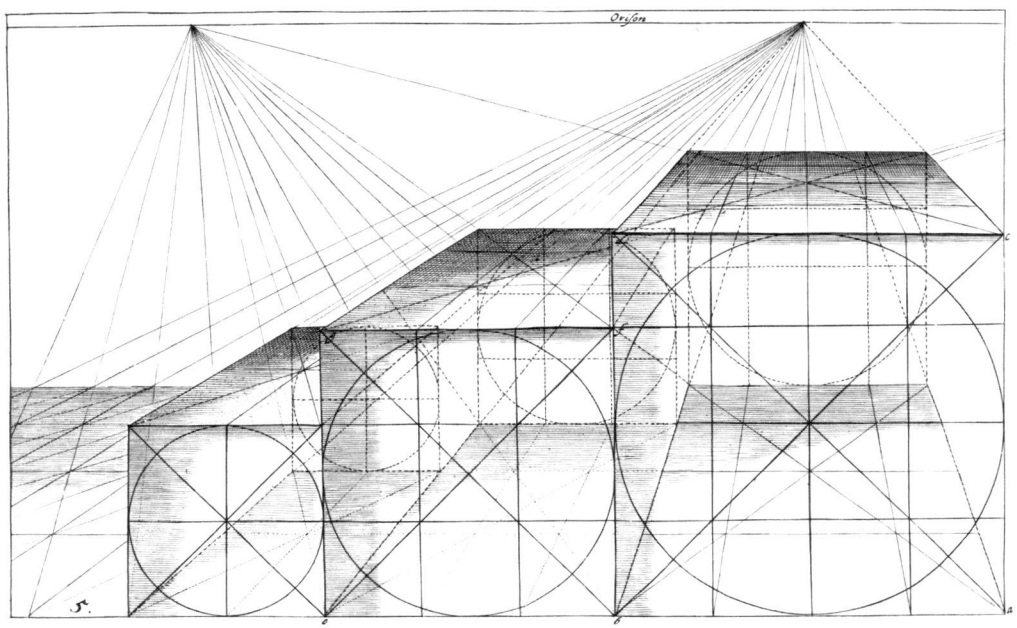

HANS VREDEMAN DE VRIES, PERSPECTIVE, PART 1: PLATE 5, *LEIDEN*, 1604–5
PREVIOUS: NICHOLAS HILLIARD, *PORTRAIT OF HENRY PERCY*, 1590–95

TAKERO SHIMAZAKI:
POINTS OF REFERENCE

I	12
II	18
III	64
IV	100
V	126

JEREMY MUSSON:
CONVERSATIONS WITH THE PAST   34

GEOFF DYER:
ZONE DOGS   72

CORINNA DEAN:
A REPOSITORY FOR FRAGMENTS   84

ADAM RICHARDS:
VANISHING POINT   108

POINTS OF REFERENCE – I

TAKERO SHIMAZAKI: Walking through the woods and down a long path towards Nithurst, a wide, open landscape emerges and you are presented with a striking, painterly image that is absolutely breathtaking. As you walk a little further along the path and stop, the view is not quite believable. It is as if a villa you had seen in some rural region of Italy, perhaps near Vicenza, or a page from an illustrated travel book by an eighteenth-century architect, has suddenly presented itself in front of your eyes. But this dream-like view is in the South Downs National Park in Sussex, just 40 minutes or so by train from London. The boldness of the house's scale, the composition of its arched windows, and its slightly flat, collage-like relationship to its context and the nearby farm buildings make you wonder what is being presented here.

Designed and built over a ten-year period by Adam Richards for himself and his family, the house represents the culmination of an autobiographical and architectural journey. There are many references to Richards's inspirations over the years, including scenes from Andrei Tarkovsky's film *Stalker*, in which three men journey through the forbidden 'Zone' in search of a room that grants a person's deepest wishes. Palladio's Villa Barbaro and Robert Mangold's abstract artworks are here too, and a reminiscence of Sir John Vanbrugh's halls and palaces.

You don't need to recognise the references, of course, to find the house very powerful. Its sheer volume and form, together with its positioning in the landscape, make this sculptural monolith an enigmatic force to appreciate, admire and equally to come to terms with.

i

POINTS OF REFERENCE — II

TAKERO SHIMAZAKI: The interior spaces are exquisitely carved out of the stepped three-storey volume and arranged around the symmetrical, 'Palladian' plan of the ground floor. The external form and facades are composed with a fascinating mix of classical, rural and contemporary architectural languages. The brickwork is full of subtle details, with patterns around the arched windows lending a sense of movement, impressively deep brick sills beneath these openings, and a darker-toned brick lattice motif on the south facade.

Curiously, though, you enter the house through a modest corner door, accessing the interior sideways via one of six concrete 'towers' that flank the main double-height space. This low-key, oblique approach seems a little contradictory to the essence of the Villa Barbaro-inspired plan, though Richards explains that he wanted to avoid grandiosity, and to create the sense of having 'chanced upon' the interior's bigger, symmetrical order. Once inside, you then encounter the main room, a magnificent, tall central chamber, cleverly arranged with kitchen and dining spaces occupying the 'void' areas between the concrete towers. A raised playroom podium at the northern end of the room adds to the classical ordering of this beautifully proportioned interior.

iii

iv

vii

CONVERSATIONS WITH THE PAST

NICOLAS POUSSIN, *LANDSCAPE WITH ST MATTHEW AND THE ANGEL*, C.1645

JEREMY MUSSON: Nithurst demonstrates notions of both what a house is and how a home should be.[1] In this case, the house is built around one principal living-kitchen room, which may be seen as a descendant of both the English medieval open hall and the *sala* of Palladio's Renaissance designs. Significantly, Nithurst was designed by an architect for occupation by himself and his family. Such houses occupy a special place in the history of domestic architecture – with pre-eminent examples being Sir John Vanbrugh's 'Goose-Pie House' in Whitehall and his miniature castle at Greenwich, as well as Sir John Soane's Museum in Lincoln's Inn Fields and his Pitzhanger Manor in Ealing. They are a particular canvas onto which architects project their life, ideas and personal dreams, and these buildings become a full demonstration of their values.[2]

As this distinctive example of humane modern architecture takes its place in the history books,[3] it is revealing to consider the character of the key room spaces at Nithurst and how they fit into a much longer history of spatial arrangement and division that could be said to emerge from the very origins of the human need for shelter, ritual and display. There have been a number of published commentaries since it was completed, which indicate that it has not only won the admiration of contemporary critics but also treads a subtle line between Modernism and Classicism.[4] This latter emphasis on style, however, does not give sufficient significance to its use, and the sense of encounter and enclosure within the key domestic spaces which constitute its plan. These spaces are defined, in part, by what has come before. Along with the technologies that make construction and sustained inhabitation possible, these ideas are fundamental to aesthetic and sensory responses to this place.

The vital importance of the way ideas and aesthetic ambitions are played out in the practical, built form is a central theme in the story of architecture. Inspired by Vitruvius's first-century CE *De Architectura*, the only treatise on architecture to survive from the ancient world, Elizabethan courtier Sir Henry Wotton argued that the true glory of the architect was to conceive of the *idea* and then make the form 'triumph over the matter'.[5] In the mid-twentieth century, architectural historian Sir Nikolaus Pevsner famously – and perhaps teasingly – tried to distinguish between architecture and a building: 'A bicycle shed is a building; Lincoln Cathedral is a piece of architecture. Nearly everything that encloses space on a scale sufficient for a human being to move in is a building; the term architecture applies only to buildings designed with a view to aesthetic appeal.'[6]

Within its striking, verdant natural surroundings, from its first appearance, Nithurst is evidently the latter. The presence of the alert, stepped and brick-faced form, in effect a low tower over a main block, enlivened

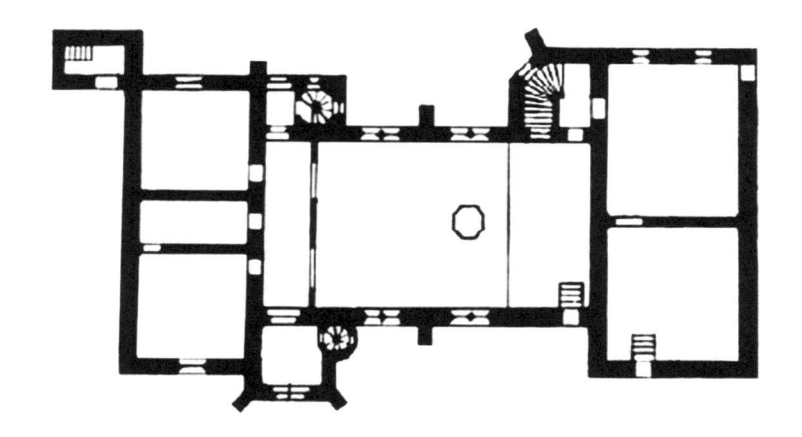

PENSHURST PLACE, KENT, C.1350

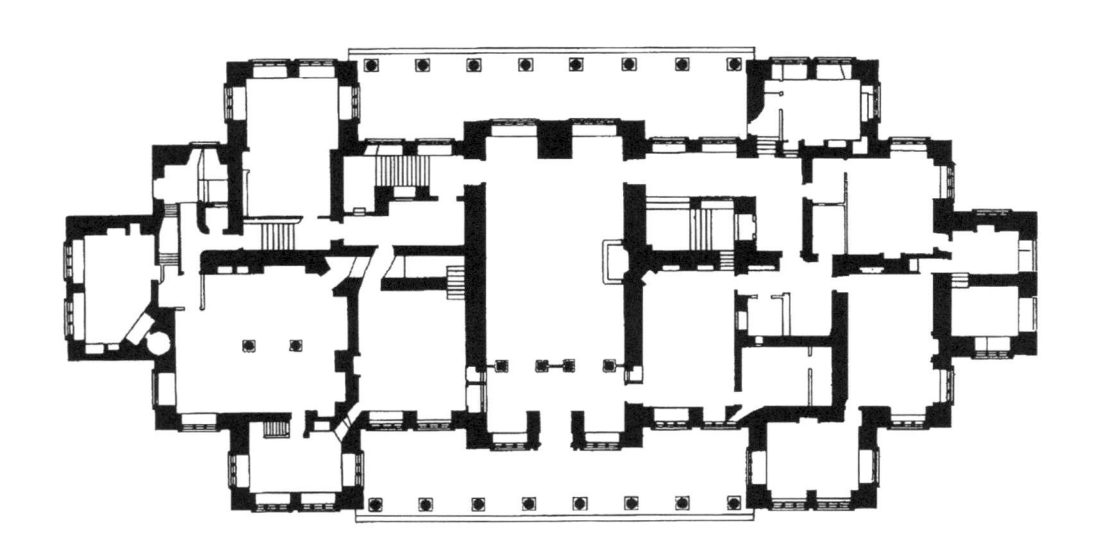

ROBERT SMYTHSON, HARDWICK HALL, DERBYSHIRE, 1590

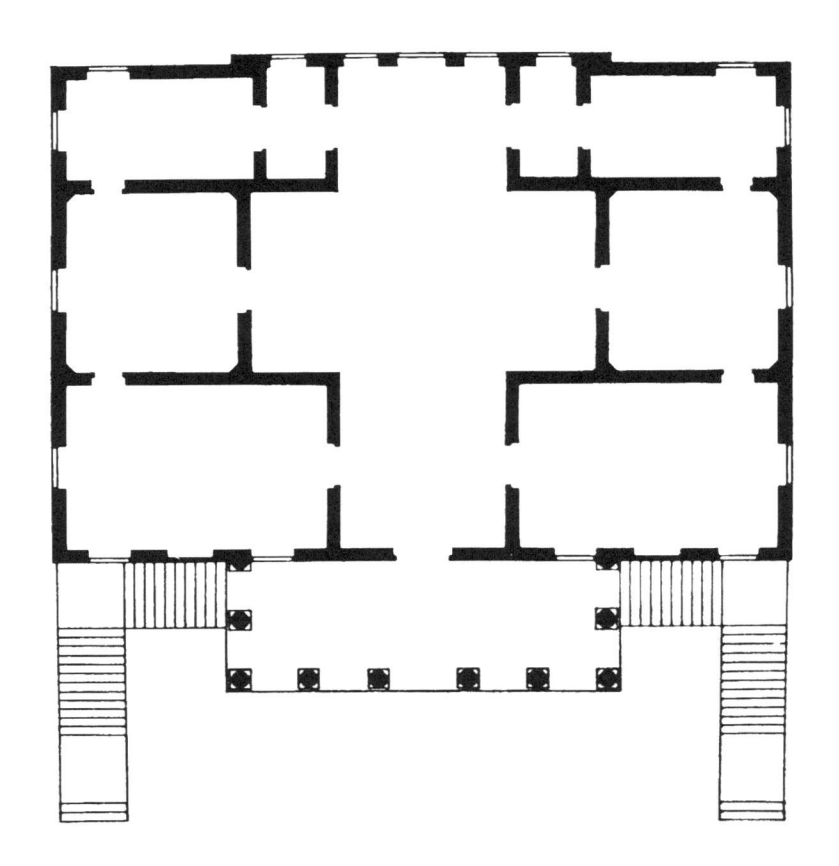

ANDREA PALLADIO, VILLA FOSCARI (VILLA 'MALCONTENTA'), VENETO, 1560

with arched windows, hints at that intrinsically historicist idea of a ruin in a landscape. It is almost suggestive of those towers in the Campagna that populate the paintings of Poussin and Claude. At the same time, the concrete inner structure within this fine outer skin in handmade brick seems to imply an industrial ruin is hidden within a Classical ruin.[7] The house thus seems to locate itself within the territory of the designed folly or eyecatcher in the English landscaped park, as well as in the post-industrial age from which it springs.

A kind of cultural archaeology is also implied in the layered, complex design and plan form of the house, which began with a careful study of the site: its landscape, field system, hedgerows and orchard terraces set around an old farmworker's cottage and small barn.[8] The much-altered, modest cottage was replaced, and the clay tile roofed barn retained. The remote-feeling site has the quality of an island in a sea of fields, surrounded by woodland – a happily secluded world. The local architectural context is expressed in a range of referenced buildings: the Tower at nearby Pitshill and Petworth Park's Monument on the hill above, as well as distinctive types of local estate cottages and barns.

This implied archaeology goes further than a considered sense of place. While entirely contemporary, the house is layered with the rational volumes and planes that evoke the Classical tradition, following the architecture of ancient Rome. There is also something of the deep-rooted solidity, practicality and strong enclosure found in the medieval hall-house tradition, and beyond into those Renaissance revisitings of the Classical past, which often blended the medieval into something distinctive and new, in which the atrium or external entrance court merged with the interior hall.

It is interesting to discover that the design of Nithurst, its relationship to the landscape and its internal sightlines and volumes were, in part, developed out of research into sixteenth-century studies by artist and architect Hans Vredeman de Vries (1527–1607). His published architectural drawings – beginning with *Scenographiae sive Perspectivae* (1560) – were not studies of actual places but idealised contrivances, invented views of cities and buildings shown in meticulously conceived linear perspectives from different viewpoints.[9]

Partly as a result of these explorations in perspectival framings, Nithurst, when seen across the fields from the steep western approach, emerges as what appears at first to be a familiar farmstead-like form, before resolving into something less distinct and familiar, more castellar, like a small fort or Claudian tower. At this point, the solid, brick structures of the Roman world are tantalisingly hinted at, with the 'Diocletian' half-circle windows – a form associated with the great public bath complexes of Imperial Rome.

Closer to the house, the sense of the order and stateliness of Roman architecture dissolves. The building is entered almost obliquely through a modest entrance hall at the north-west end – a device that can be noted in the work of Edwin Lutyens. The compression of this entrance adds to a thrilling encounter with the high-ceilinged living-kitchen, which is 4.5 metres high.

This is a central experience of the house, and a key to its particular plan, as well as to its place in architectural history. The form of this great room clearly draws partly on the model of the medieval, multi-purpose 'open' hall of the smaller manor house kind, then in effect the only real room of the house.[10] In the long medieval period, the hall was used for life: dining, ritual, celebration, business and administration, and although services, kitchens and serveries were adjacent and not originally integrated, some of the household probably slept in the room.[11] Over time the service areas became more integrated within the structure of the house, and hall and kitchen carefully paired in the architecture. The ancient and long-lasting central hall was effectively demoted in the later seventeenth and eighteenth centuries to become a more formalised entrance space. However, from the beginnings of the Gothic Revival era, when it had particular social and historicist connotations, it was revived as a feature of the domestic design of the country house; but even then Sir George Gilbert Scott referred to how it might serve as 'a delightful sitting room, especially in the summer'.[12]

As Mark Girouard observed, 'this potentiality of the great hall' was to be taken up by influential architects such as William Eden Nesfield and Richard Norman Shaw. This potentiality heralded the living-halls which had a significant place in the Arts and Crafts domestic plan and the Edwardian country house generally. Hermann Muthesius, in *Das englische Haus* (1904–5), wrote about how the revived hall had become 'a room of so pleasing and impressive a form [that it] could not but attract some part of the life of the house to itself', and noted how in some new country houses it effectively replaced the drawing room.[13]

At Nithurst, the hall tradition importantly combines with the twenty-first-century version of the Modernist open-plan, a type normally traced from the inventive 'prairie house' architecture of Frank Lloyd Wright, in 1909, at Robie House, Hyde Park, Chicago.[14] In essence, the living-kitchen at Nithurst is a generationally integrated family room, where cooking, feasting, studying and talking happen together in the same space. In a subtle inversion of the medieval tradition, where the upper end of the hall would feature a dais for the head of the household, the room has a raised platform looking down on the kitchen and out to farmland which serves as a capacious children's playroom. Opposite, at the south end

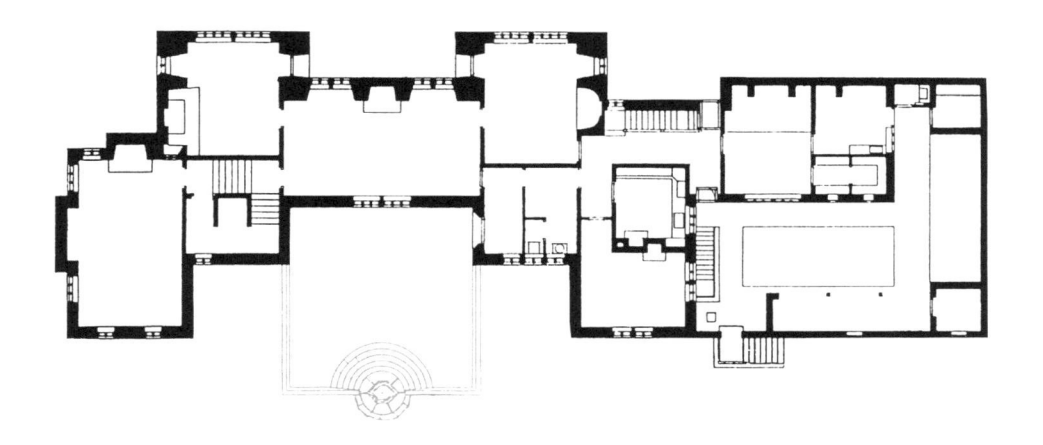

EDWIN LUTYENS, BARTON ST MARY, WEST SUSSEX, 1906

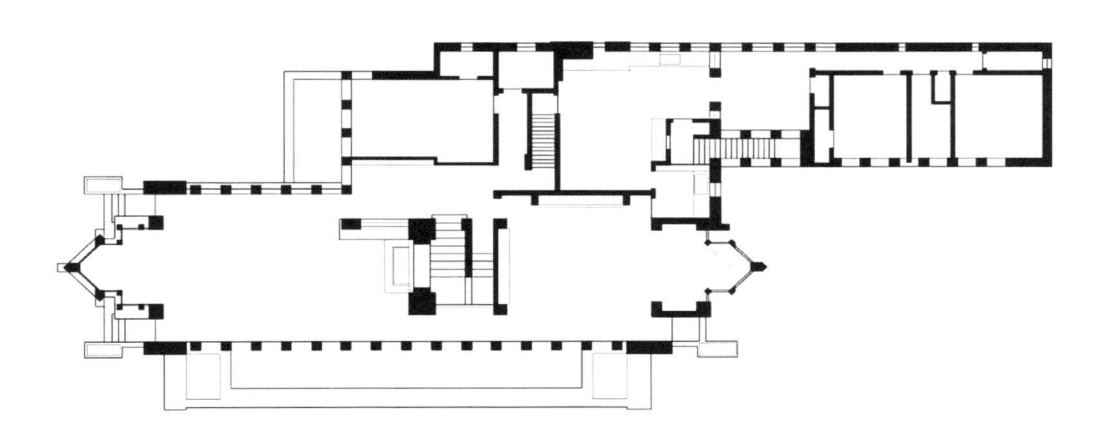

FRANK LLOYD WRIGHT, ROBIE HOUSE, CHICAGO, 1909

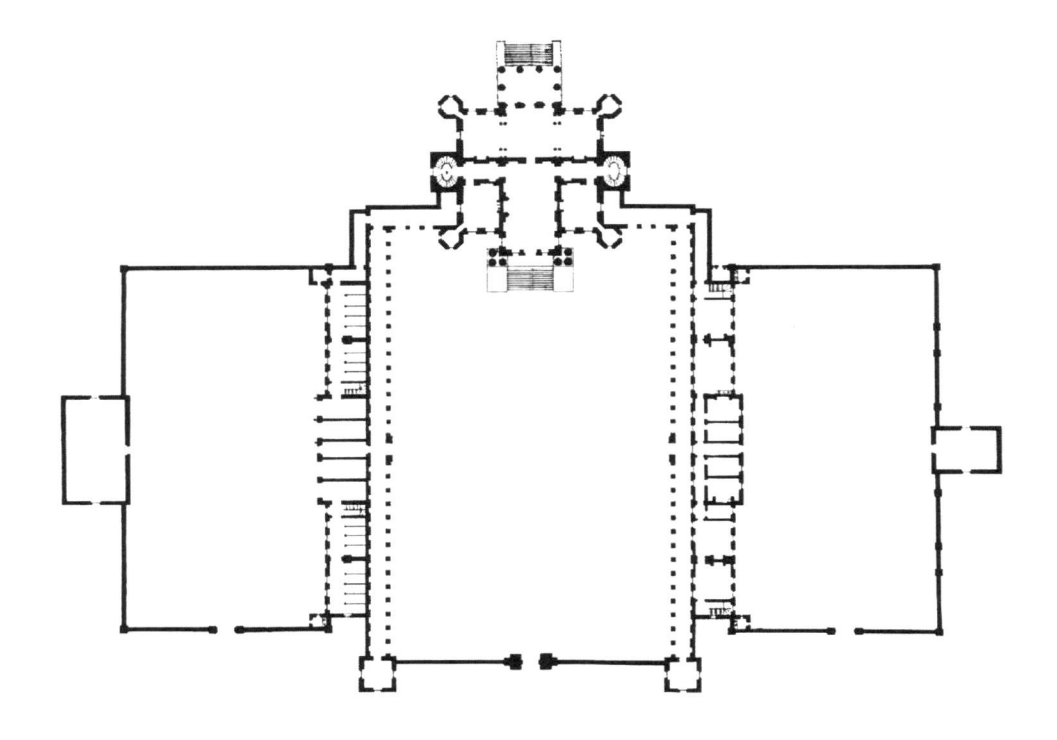

JOHN VANBRUGH, SEATON DELAVAL HALL, NORTHUMBERLAND, 1728

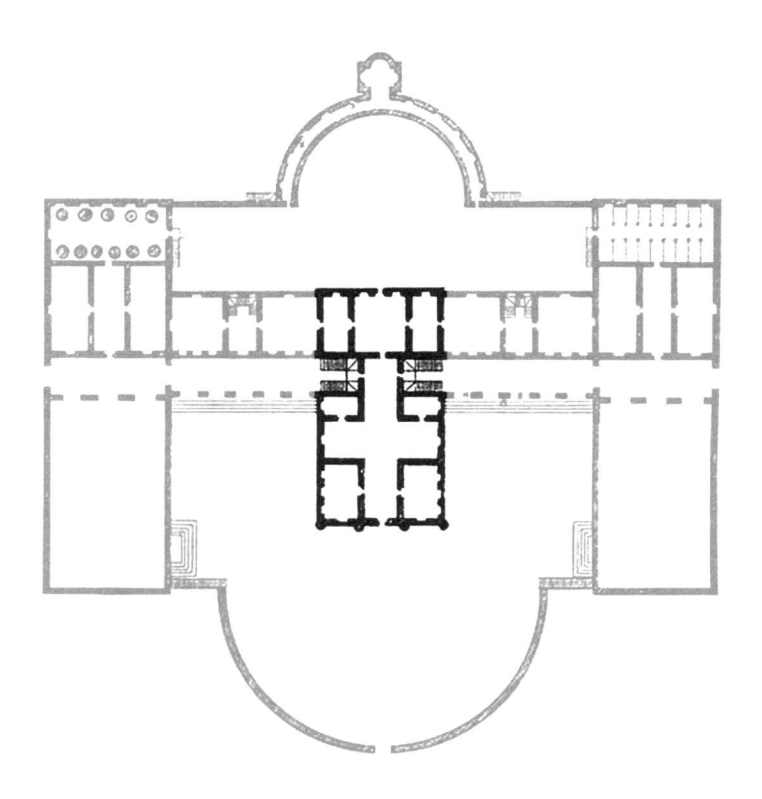

ANDREA PALLADIO, VILLA BARBARO, VENETO, 1570

of the room, is a gallery that allows people on the first floor to look down into the living-kitchen.

Vanbrugh's house plans often used this connection between the first-floor gallery and the principal hall (for instance, Castle Howard, Seaton Delaval Hall) to provide, in part, a viewing point over the life below, as at Nithurst. This was different from the traditional medieval arrangement but, interestingly, it is how the hall at the 1590s Hardwick Hall worked,[15] a house which Vanbrugh appears to have visited.

The high-ceilinged, light-filled space of this kitchen-living room flows around six internal towers. These clasp to the external walls, creating an unexpected sense of depth, and the feeling of standing within some ancient, thick-walled building. In practical terms, these towers create useful enclosed areas that are distinct from the main space, as well as playing their own part in the exploration of ideas which the house invites. At Nithurst, the walls and ceilings of the inner frame are left as unfinished concrete, creating a striking and modern effect for this interior.

The squared-off presence of these internal towers perhaps reconnects to the echoes of Roman forts first noted on the western approach. This articulation of the space also links the house to the ground plan of Palladio's Villa Barbaro. As published in *I Quattro Libri*, in 1570,[16] Palladio's plan of the Villa Barbaro has the curious and engaging quality of seeming to outline a miniaturised city within a villa, a way of life in microcosm.

Built near Vicenza in 1557–8, the villa was commissioned by the two Barbaro brothers and absorbed part of an old family *castello* within its structure. It was also noted for its elongated composition: a central wing with various side pavilions, and courtyards, barns and dovecotes, the central cruciform *sala* forming an especially resonant space, enlivened by murals by Paolo Veronese. Simon Schama called this interior space 'the dreamscape ... a perfect slice of Renaissance escapism'.[17]

One of the two brothers, the cleric Daniele Barbaro, was Palladio's second most important mentor after the Count Gian Giorgio Trissino. In 1556 Daniele Barbaro published his translation and commentary on Vitruvius – with illustrations by Palladio. This somehow re-evident cultural intimacy reinforces the impression given by the Villa Barbaro that its design emerged out of a dialogue of ideas about the architecture of the Classical world as seen through Renaissance eyes: a building as a conversation with the past.

The *sala* of a Palladian villa plan – which influenced the plan of Nithurst via the model of the Villa Barbaro – played a key architectural role in establishing the controlling symmetry and language of the whole. The *sala* emerged from medieval precedents of the hall, and as Palladio himself wrote, served for 'feasts, entertainments and decorations, for comedies, weddings and such like recreations'.[18] Always designed as a high space, the *sala* created a distinctive sense of depth that is recalled by the airy height of Nithurst's kitchen-living room.

Intriguingly, the deep window recessions between the internal towers are almost rooms within rooms: one a kitchen space, the other, in effect, a breakfast room, while those to the north serve as entrance lobbies and additional space to the dining area. These recessions are, in some ways, reminiscent of the oriels of medieval manor houses.[19] The scale of the oriel windows was not only practical but also a significant indicator of status. The light that flooded the dais end of the medieval manor falls more democratically at Nithurst, across both high end and low.

The principal sitting room faces south, which echoes the historical location of the great chamber in relation to a hall in a medieval residence,[20] raised and separate from the hall but close and interconnected by function and ritual. It has a large, tripartite window arrangement opening to the lawn, but here the 'status' is only the privilege of privacy in a spacious room that enjoys good light and views, which connect the occupant to the stepped landscape outside.

The overall plan is admirably compact and interconnected. The living-kitchen and the sitting room are the principal ground-floor spaces and a short stair to the west leads from the former to the latter, while a compact staircase to the east rises to the first floor and the family and guest bedrooms.[21] Bedrooms are ingeniously served by bathrooms concealed within the upper sections of those internal towers rising from the living-kitchen below. From the landing and through double doors, there is a steep staircase leading to the master bedroom suite, on the uppermost floor.

This final layer – in effect the upper part of a three-storey tower – allows the south elevation to read as an alert, playful turret, a deliberate echo of the 1717 brick-built belvedere designed by Vanbrugh for the Duke of Newcastle, at Claremont in Surrey.[22] The rest of the house recedes playfully behind this when viewed from the long narrow lawn formed on a former orchard terrace.

The unusual, tapered plan of Nithurst affects responses to the house from within and without. Elizabethan and Jacobean designers took pleasure in 'conceits' or 'devices', the use of geometrical shapes or patterns in ground plans that are enjoyable and elegant in their own right.[23] These shaped and inventive structures – such as the 1590s Triangular Lodge at Rushton, in Northamptonshire – reflected a key moment in the evolution of English architecture when the idea met the real in architectural form.

Writing about the evolution of modern architecture, William Curtis pointed to 'a personal language that crystallizes features of its period and society'

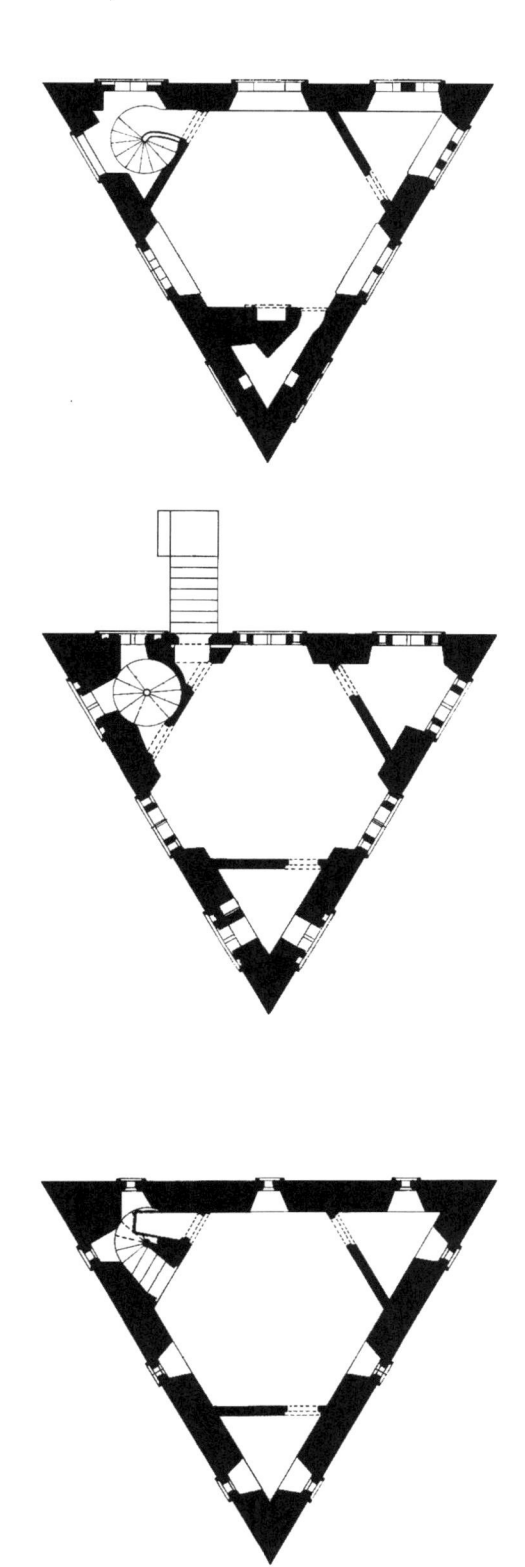

TRIANGULAR LODGE AT RUSHTON, NORTHAMPTONSHIRE, C.1590S

JOHN THORPE, DRAWING FOR A CIRCULAR HOUSE

but he also observed that 'the more interesting the individual creation, the harder it is to locate it in a particular chronological slot'.[24] Nithurst is just such an individual creation, expressing a series of traditional treatments of space and form in its contemporary design. It is a book of architecture in itself, threaded through with an understanding of the deeper history of domestic architecture, but these threads are drawn together and resolved in unexpected and unconventional ways to both subtle and memorable effect.

1. Jeremy Musson, 'Stairway to Heaven: Nithurst Farm', *Country Life*, 5 August 2020, pp 76–81. The author visited the house both during construction and after completion, a privileged encounter for the architectural historian.
2. ibid., p.80.
3. Ian Nairn, Elizabeth Williamson, Tim Hudson, Jeremy Musson, *Buildings of England: Sussex West*, Yale University Press, London, 2019, p.658.
4. Rob Wilson, 'One for the Ages: Nithurst Farm by Adam Richards', *Architectural Journal*, 6 November 2019.
5. Mark Girouard, *Elizabethan Architecture: Its Rise and Fall*, Yale University Press, London, 2009, p.57.
6. Nikolaus Pevsner, *An Outline of European Architecture*, revised edition, Penguin Books, London, 1974, p.15.
7. Wilson, 'One for the Ages', 2019.
8. Musson, 'Stairway to Heaven', 2020, pp 78–80.
9. www.doaks.org/resources/online-exhibits/hans-vredeman-de-vries, accessed 28 April 2024.
10. Charles O'Brien, *Houses: An Architectural Guide*, Yale University Press, London, 2016, pp 10–11.
11. See, for an example of the early manor house plan, Edward Impey, 'The Manor House, Boothby Pagnell', *Country Life*, 29 July 1999, pp 84–7.
12. Mark Girouard, *The Victorian Country House*, Yale University Press, New Haven, CT, 1979, p.46, quoting Scott in *Secular and Domestic Architecture*, 1857.
13. Hermann Muthesius, *The English House*, vol.II, 1904–5, pp 50–51.
14. https://flwright.org/explore/frederick-c-robie-house, accessed 25 April 2024; and William J.R. Curtis, *Modern Architecture since 1900*, revised edition, Phaidon, London, 2016, pp 113–14, 123–5.
15. Nicholas Cooper, 'Two Hardwick Halls: Sources, Forms and Intentions', and 'New Hall: Realising Intentions', in David Adshead, ed., *Hardwick Hall: A Great Old Castle of Romance*, Yale University Press, London, 2016, pp 1–17, p.7 and pp 19–38, p.23 respectively.
16. Andrea Palladio, *The Four Books of Architecture*, 1570, as translated by Giacomo Leoni, 1738, plate 34 and p.49.
17. Quoted in Dr Laura Moretti, 'How the Barbaro Brothers Created the Perfect Renaissance Villa', British Academy blog, 23 March 2018, https://www.thebritishacademy.ac.uk/blog/how-barbaro-brothers-created-perfect-renaissance-villa/, accessed 25 April 2024.
18. Andrea Palladio, *The Four Books of Architecture*, 1570, ch.xxi, p.27 (in the translation published by Isaac Ware, 1738).
19. Mark Girouard, *Life in the English Country House*, Yale University Press, New Haven, CT, 1979, pp 34–40; and John Goodall, *The English Castle 1066–1650*, Yale University Press, New Haven, CT, 2011, pp 24–7.
20. Girouard, *Life*, 1979, pp 44–6.
21. Musson, 'Stairway to Heaven', 2020, p.80.
22. Jeremy Musson, *The Country Houses of Sir John Vanbrugh*, Aurum Press, London, 2011, pp 153–4; and Howard Colvin, *Biographical Dictionary of British Architects, 1600–1840*, Yale University Press, London, 2008, p.1072.
23. Barbara Jones, *Follies and Grottoes*, Constable & Co, London, 1953, pp 1–7.
24. Curtis, *Modern Architecture*, 2016, p.15.

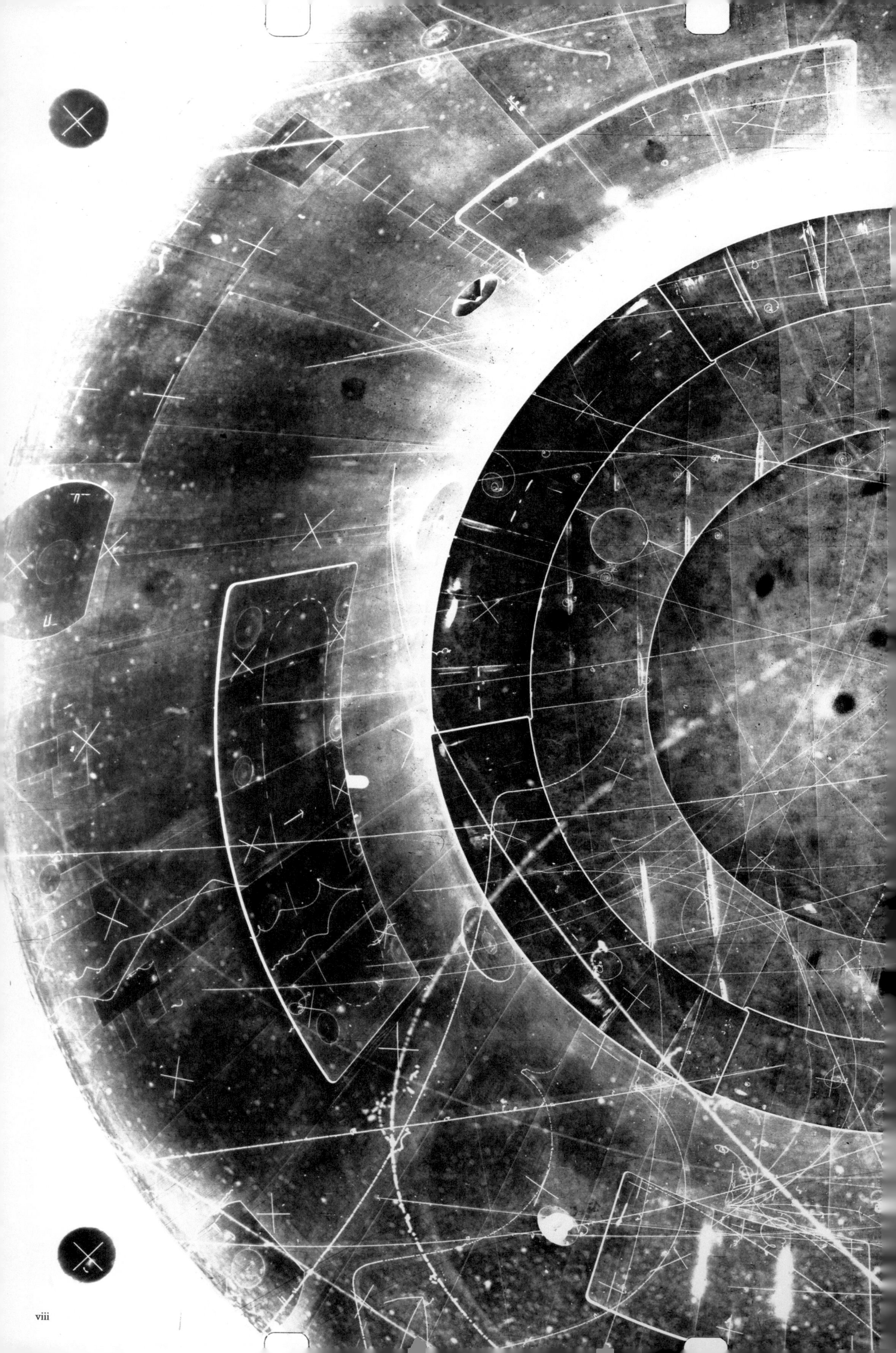

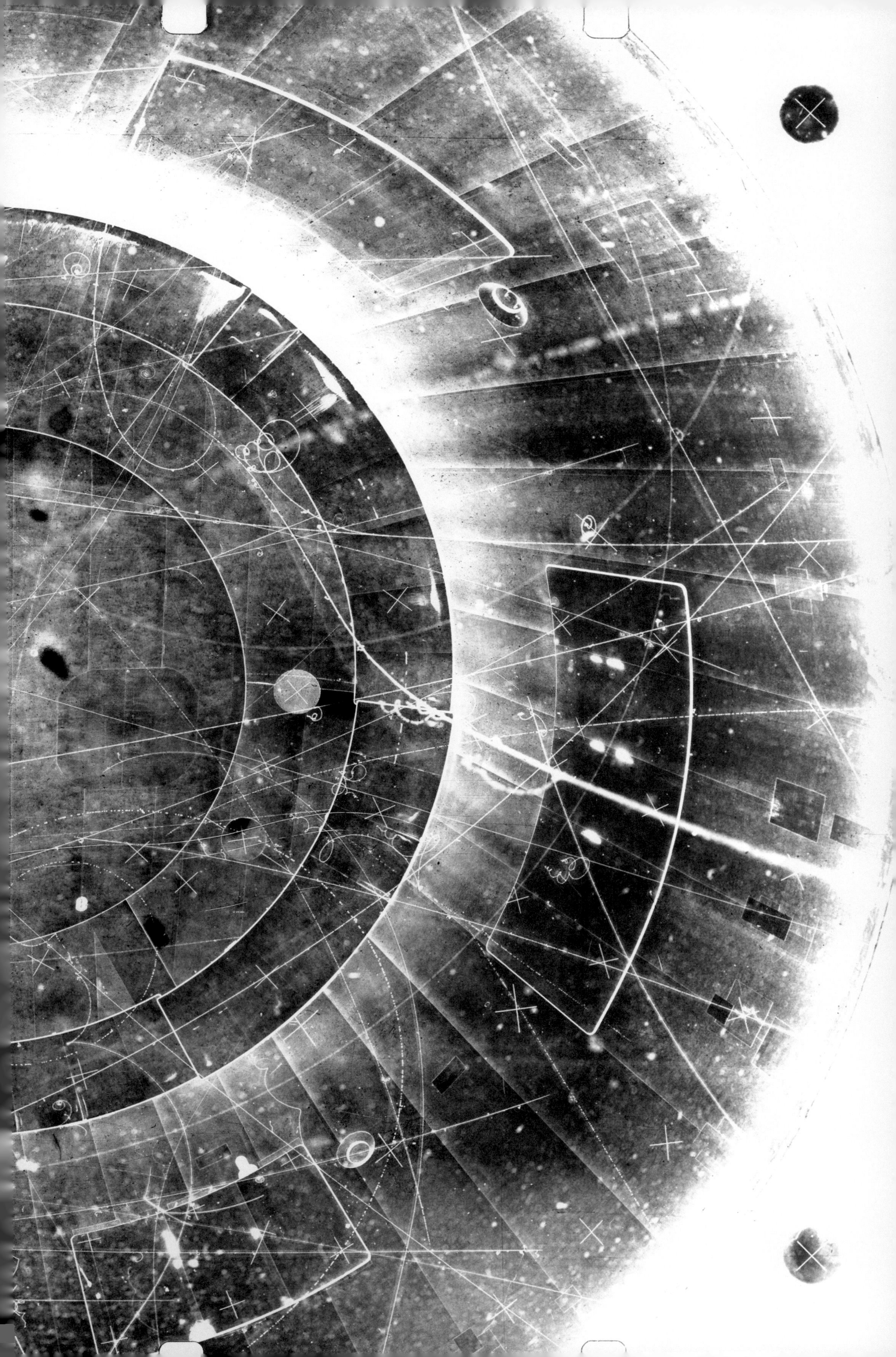

COLUBER.

Plate II.

The Lachesis, or fatal Viper.

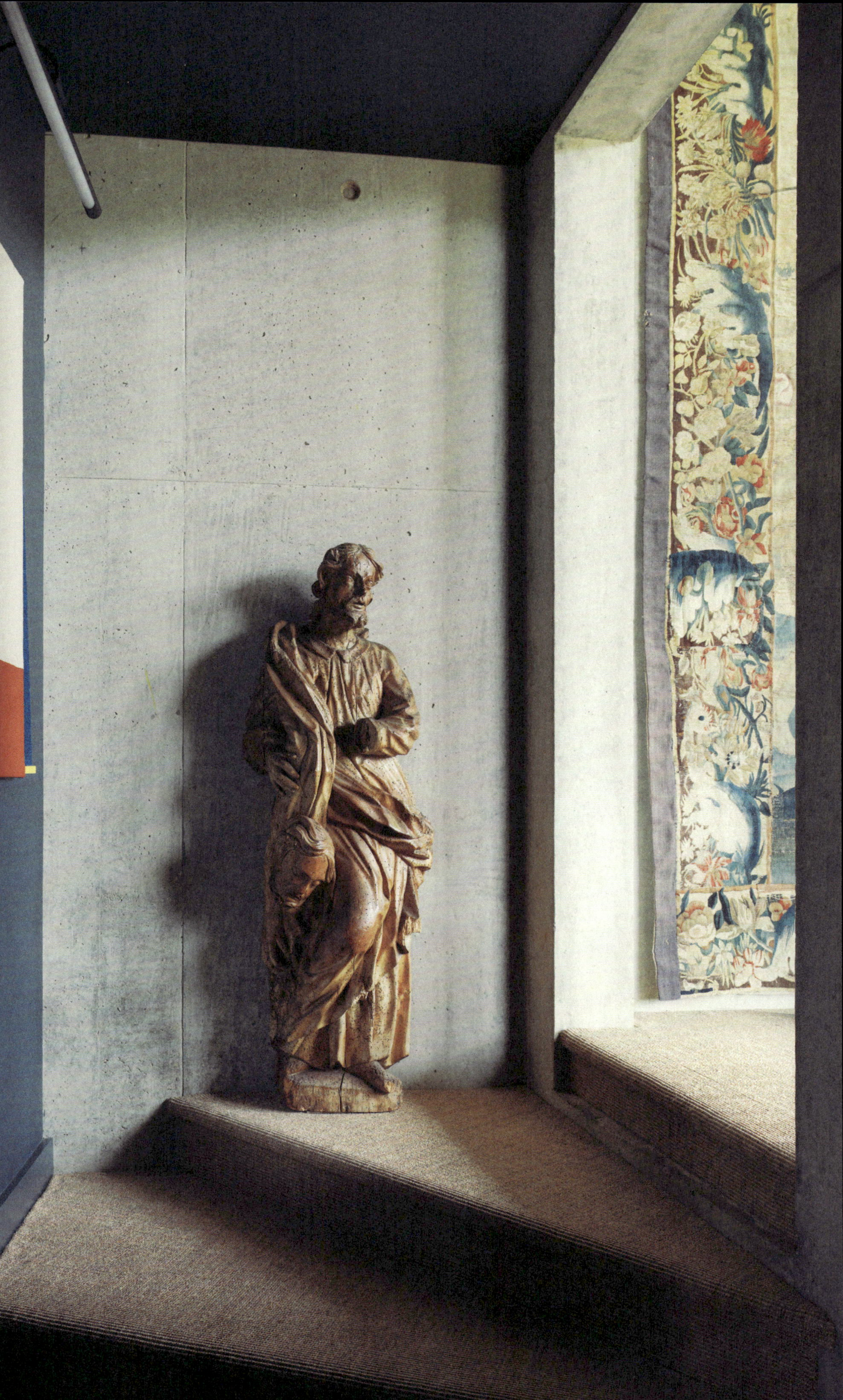

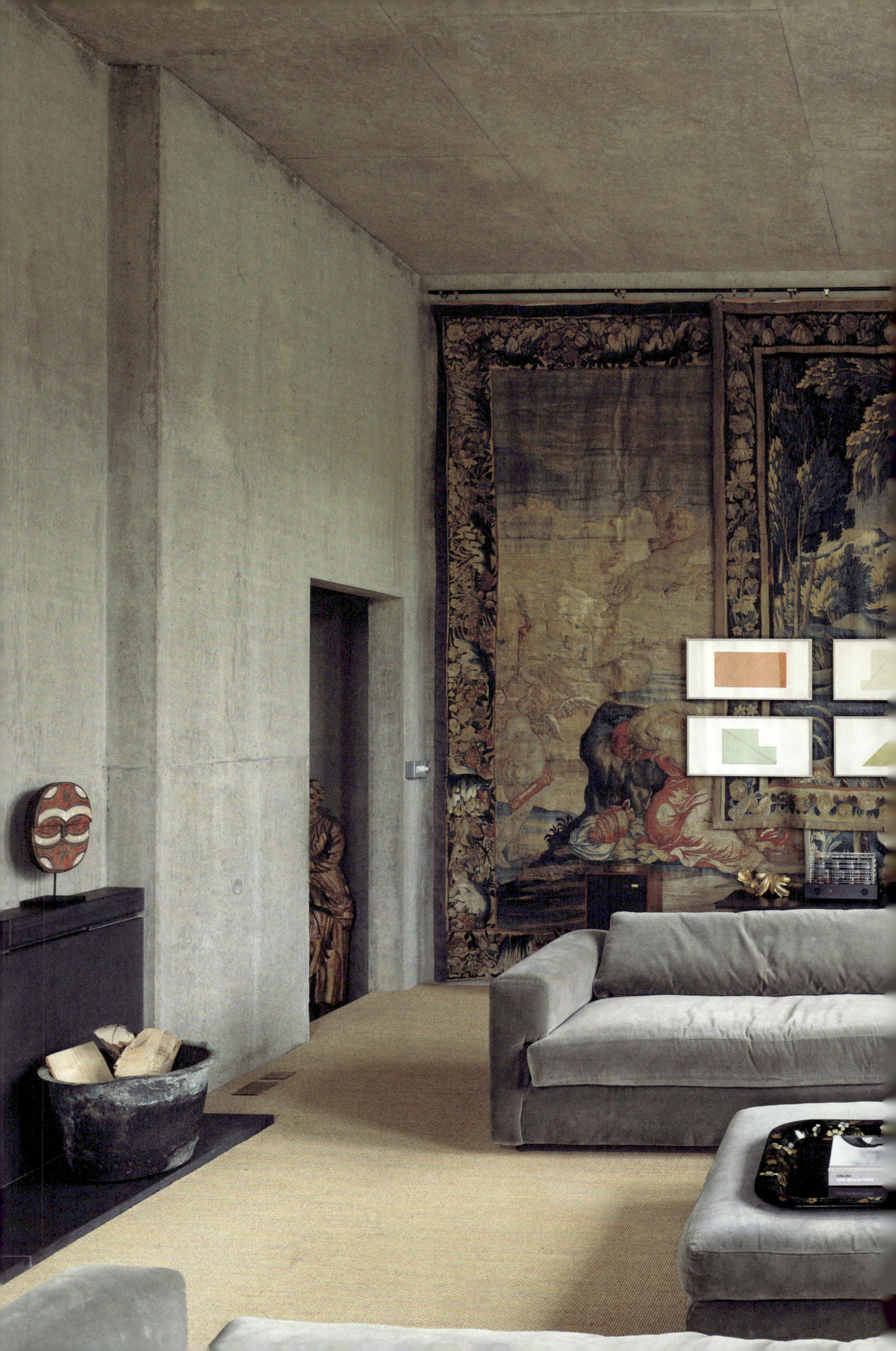

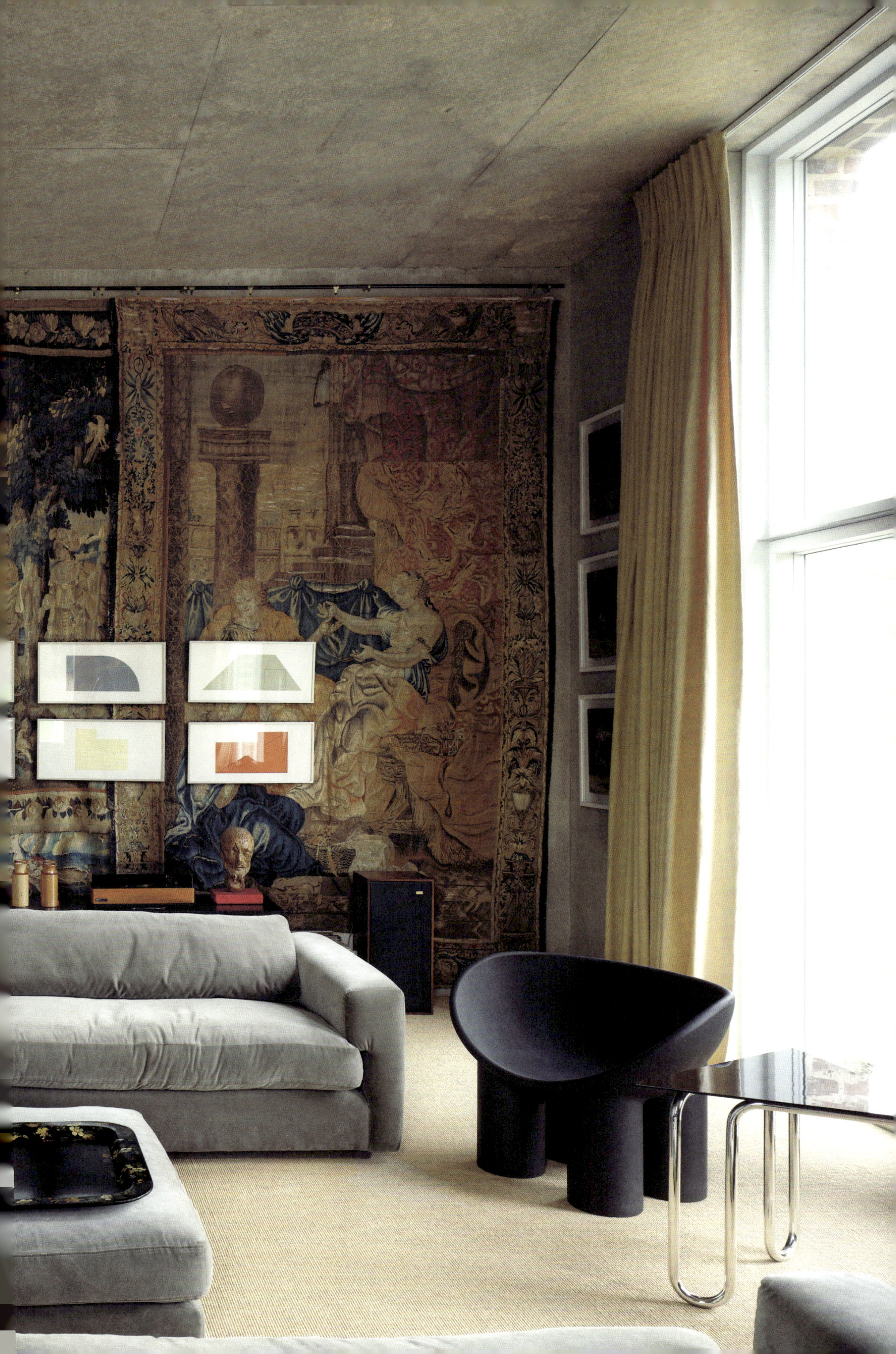

x

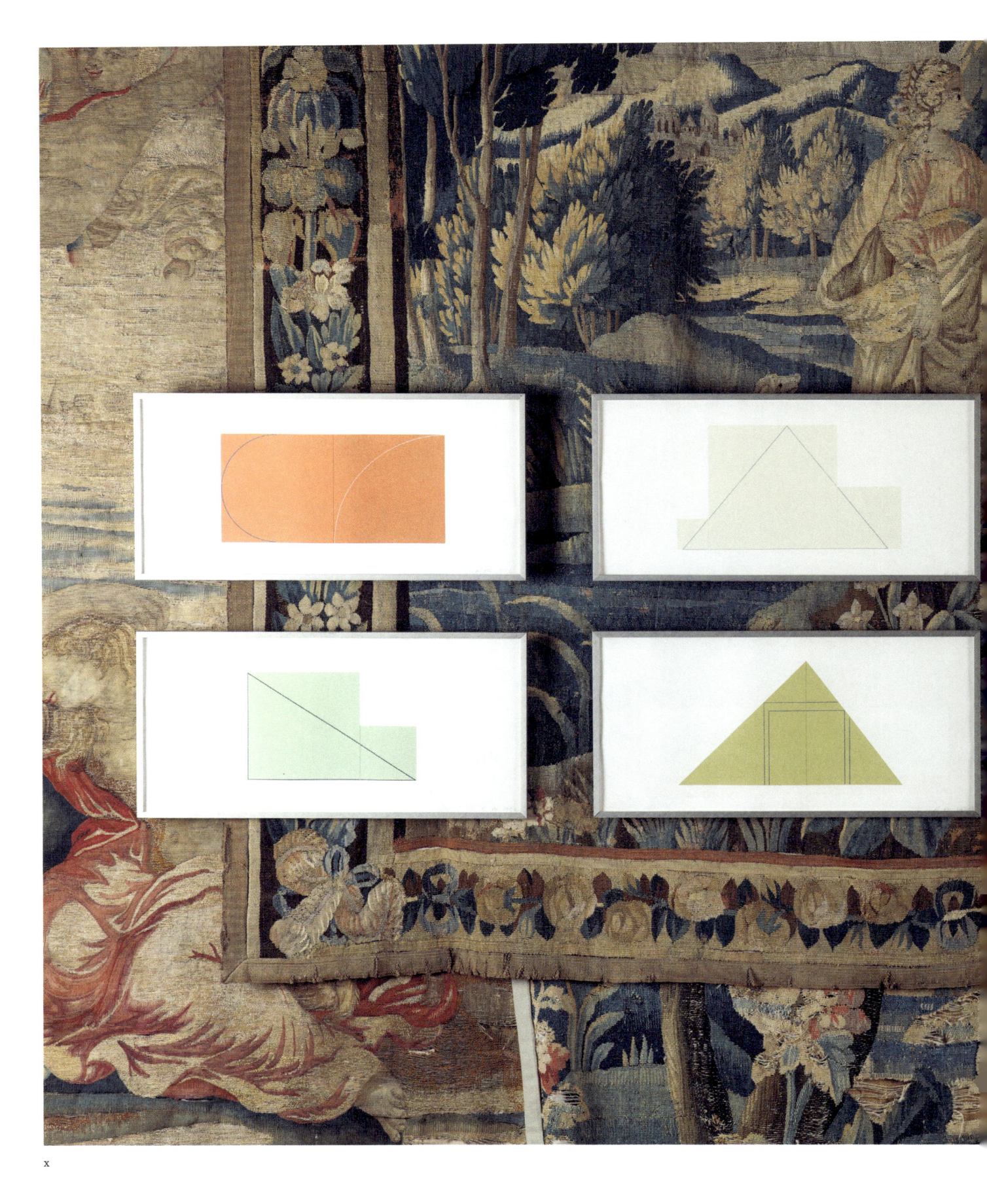

55

xi

xii

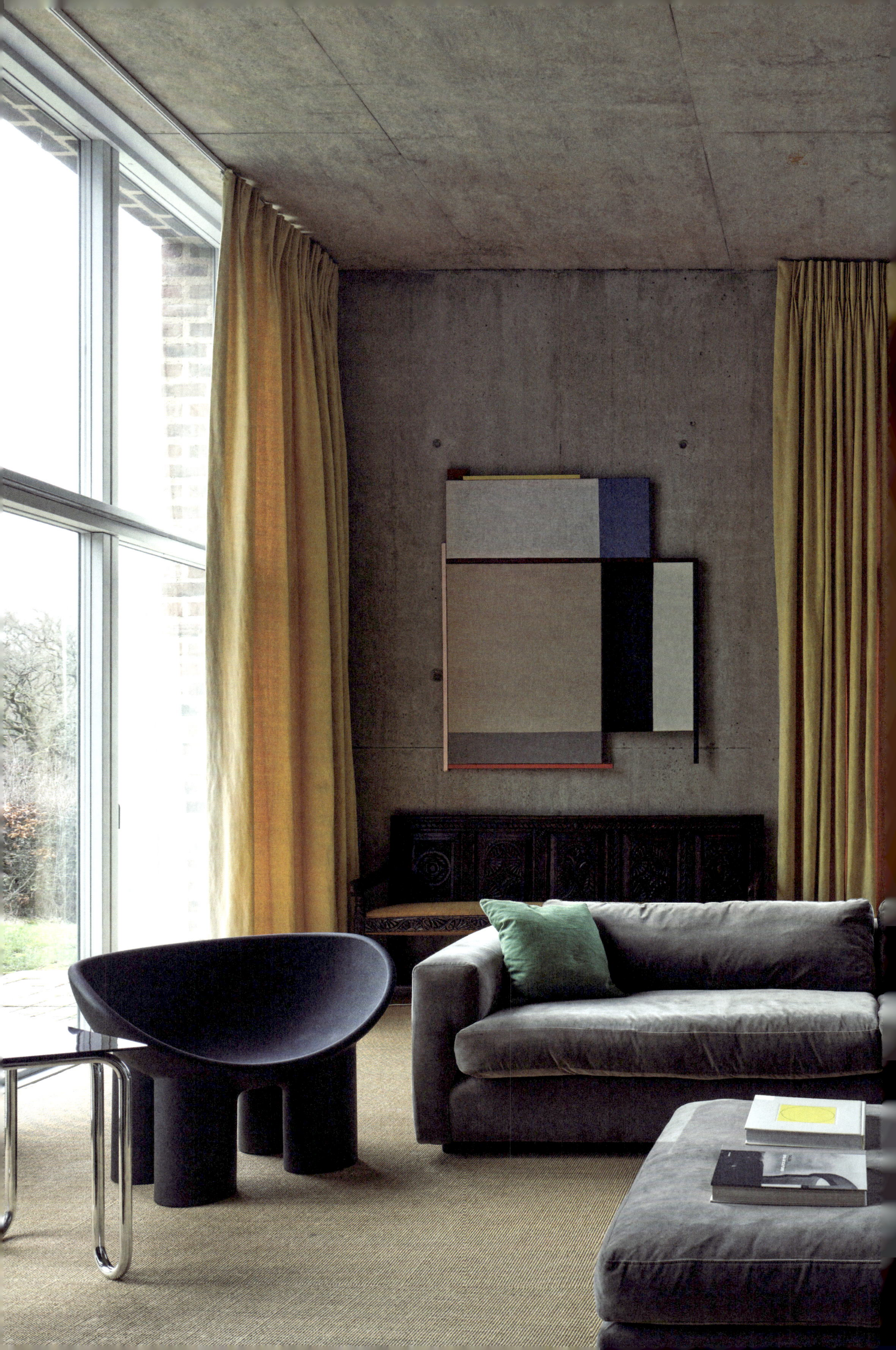

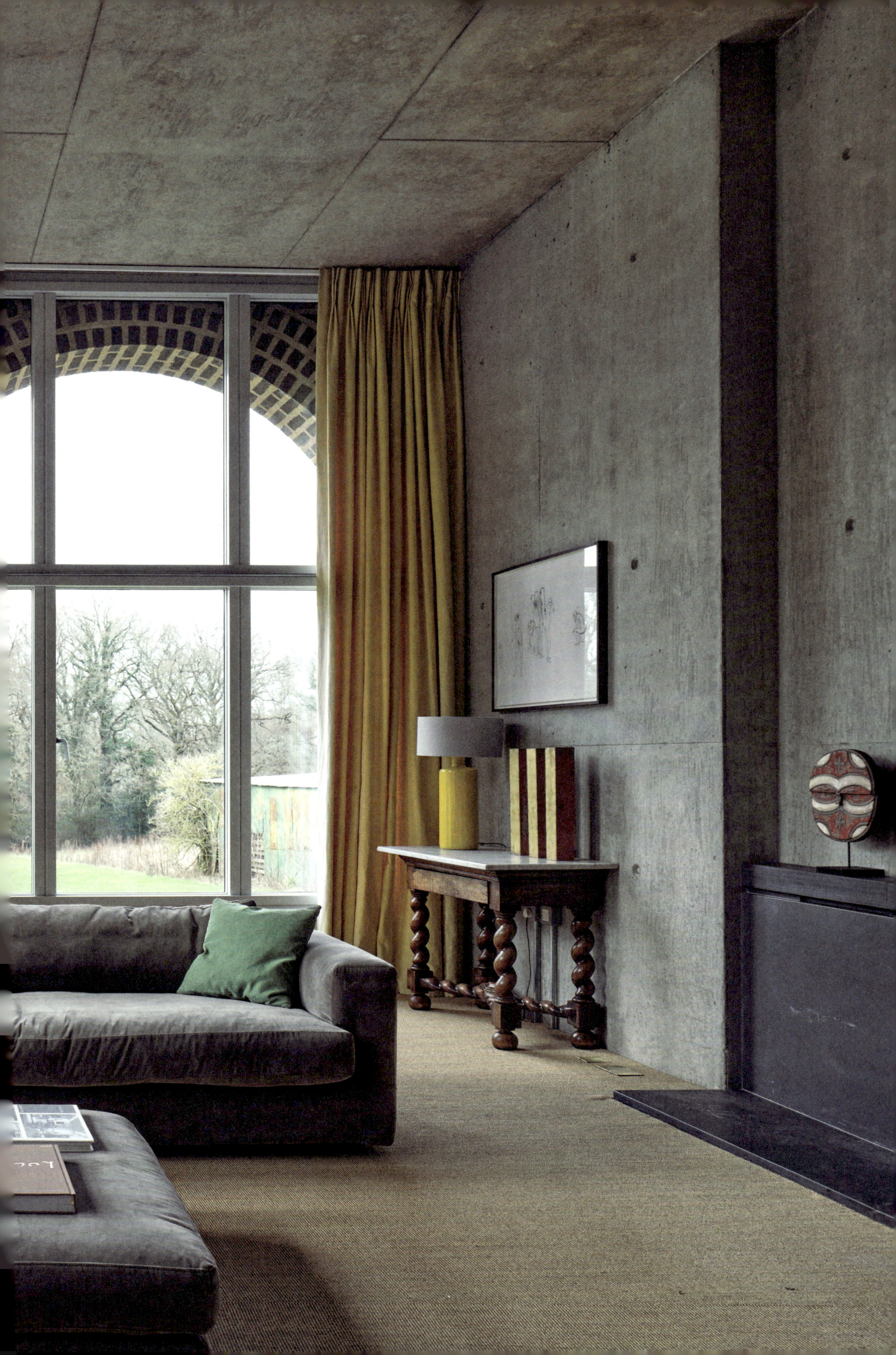

xiii

xiv

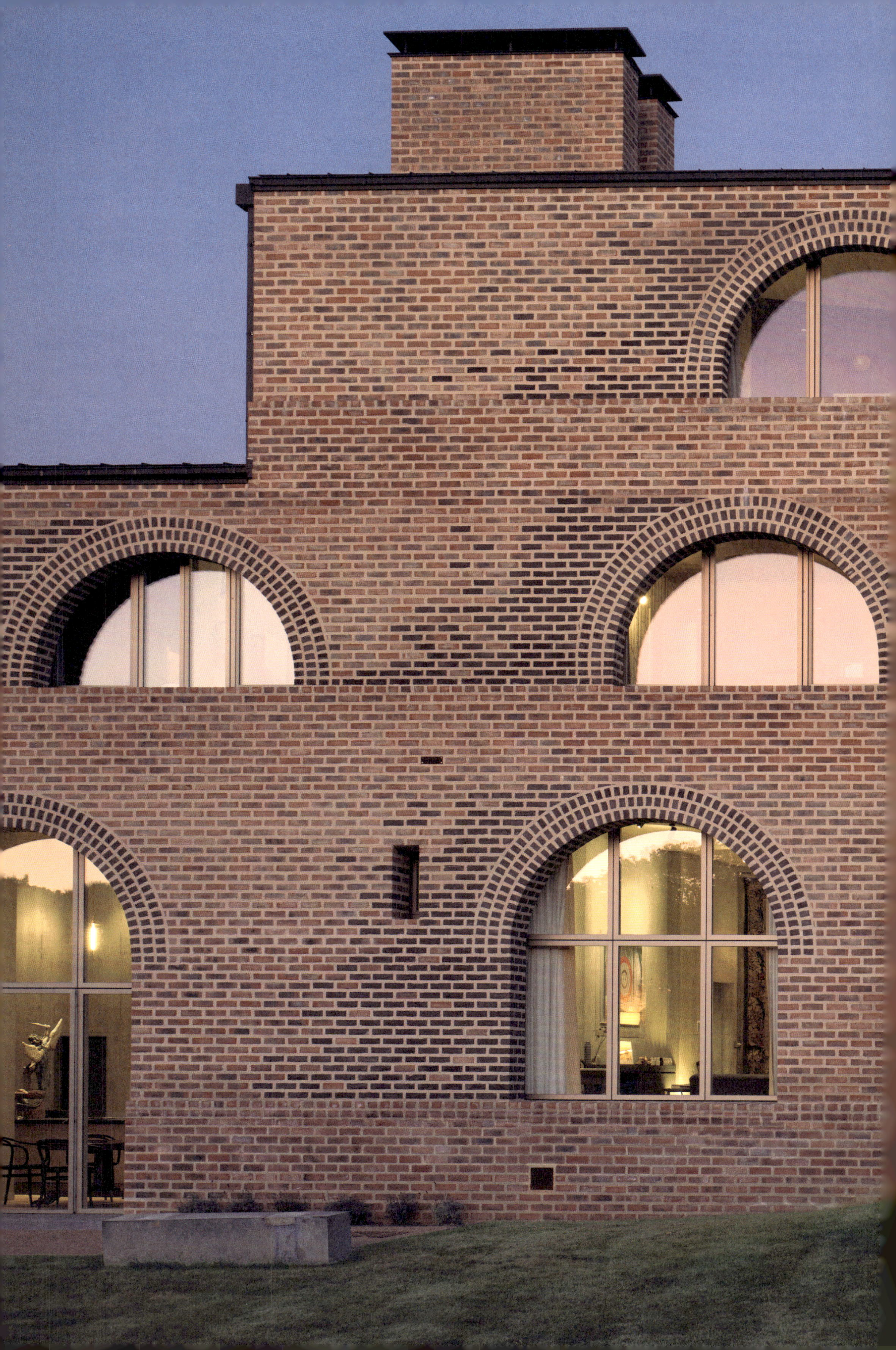

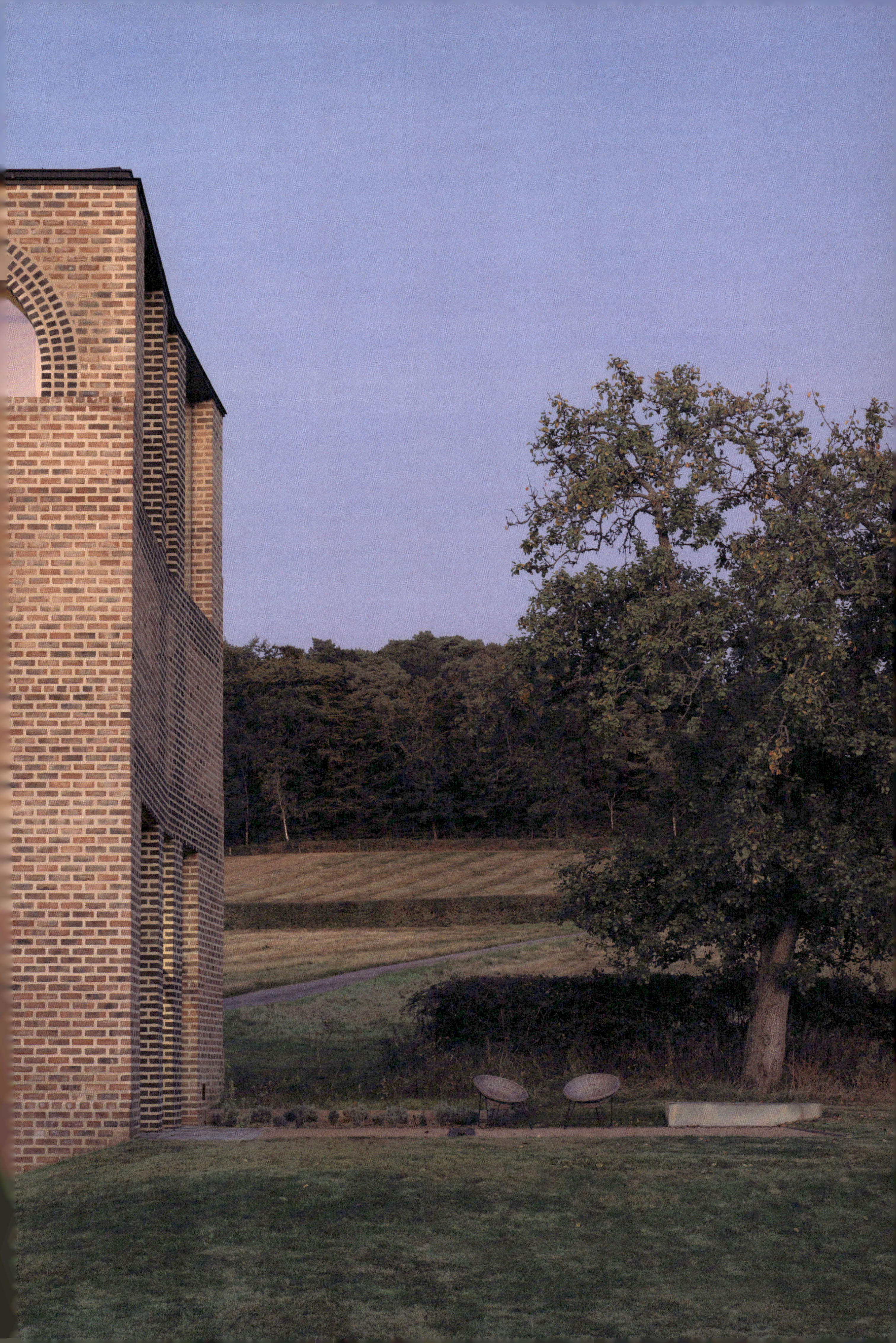

POINTS OF REFERENCE – III

TAKERO SHIMAZAKI: Richards, an engaging storyteller, evokes a scene in *Stalker* – in which the guide enters the 'Zone' with his two clients – as he leads us from the main room, through a dark, transverse stair hall to the sitting room at the south end of the house. It's a surprise to find this cosier living 'Room', whose proportions are quite different to those of the main room we have left behind. With sofas paired symmetrically in the centre, and surrounded by artworks, tapestries and books, it is an oasis of escape.

From here one can wander out to the south garden, where the lawn seems to extend out into the darkness of the woods beyond. The gentle slope of this grassed path makes the idea of a journey towards the 'Zone' quite relatable, even though we are no longer inside the house. Looking back, the south facade – perhaps the least bold – is beautifully resolved and composed with a very subtle vertical inflection at its centre. From here you begin to notice the way the entire house tapers from one end to the other in plan.

The effect of this gentle tapering takes different guises in different parts of the house. In the main room, it accentuates the magnificent nave-like view towards the entrance to the 'Room', as well as the space widening towards the glazed end by the playroom. The southerly concave facade adds ever so gently and subtly to how the building engages with the rear garden and terrace. The flatness of this facade and the darker-toned brick pattern provide a classical assurance using contemporary means, making a graphic 'eyecatcher' as you approach the house from the woods.

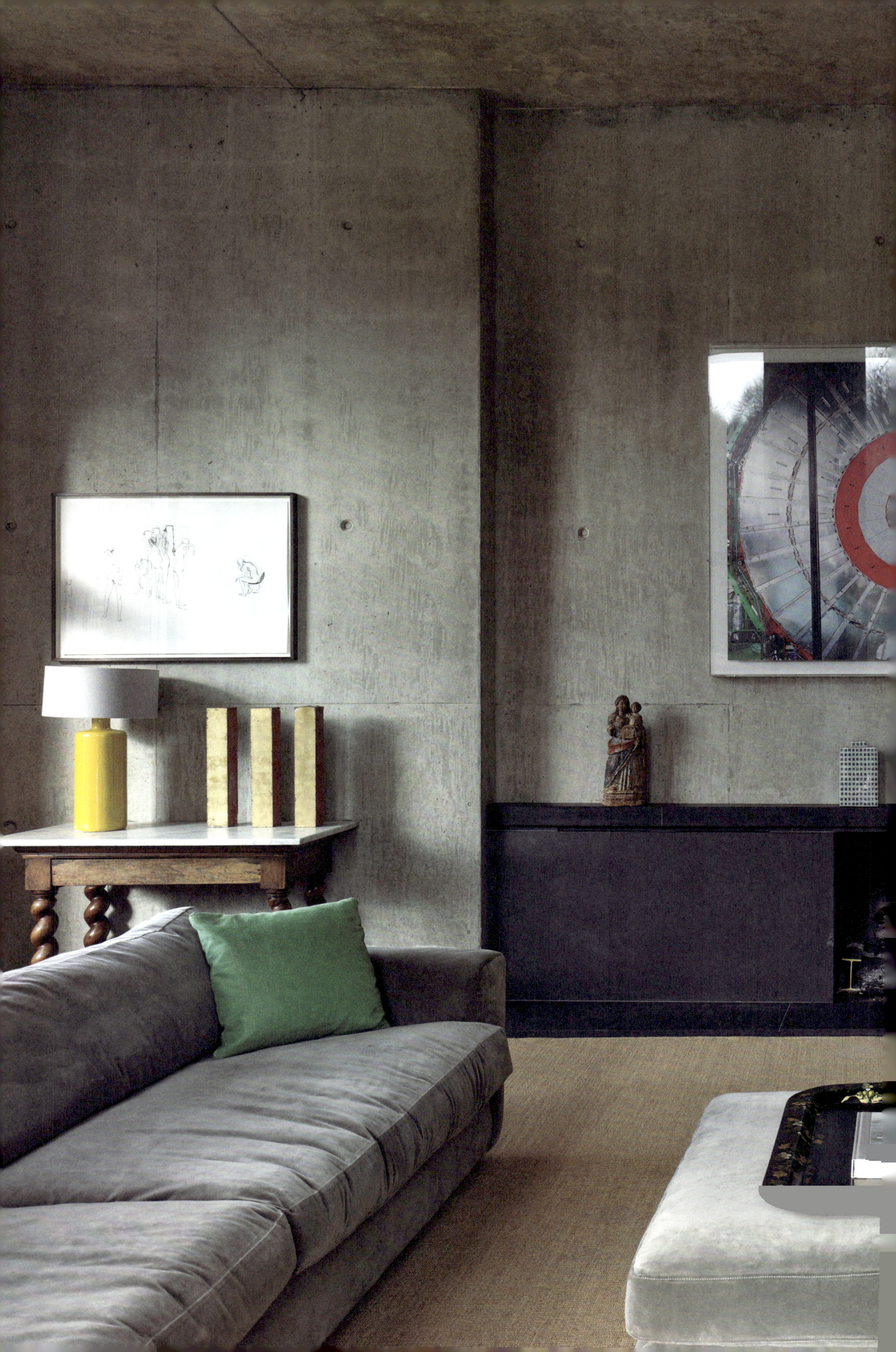

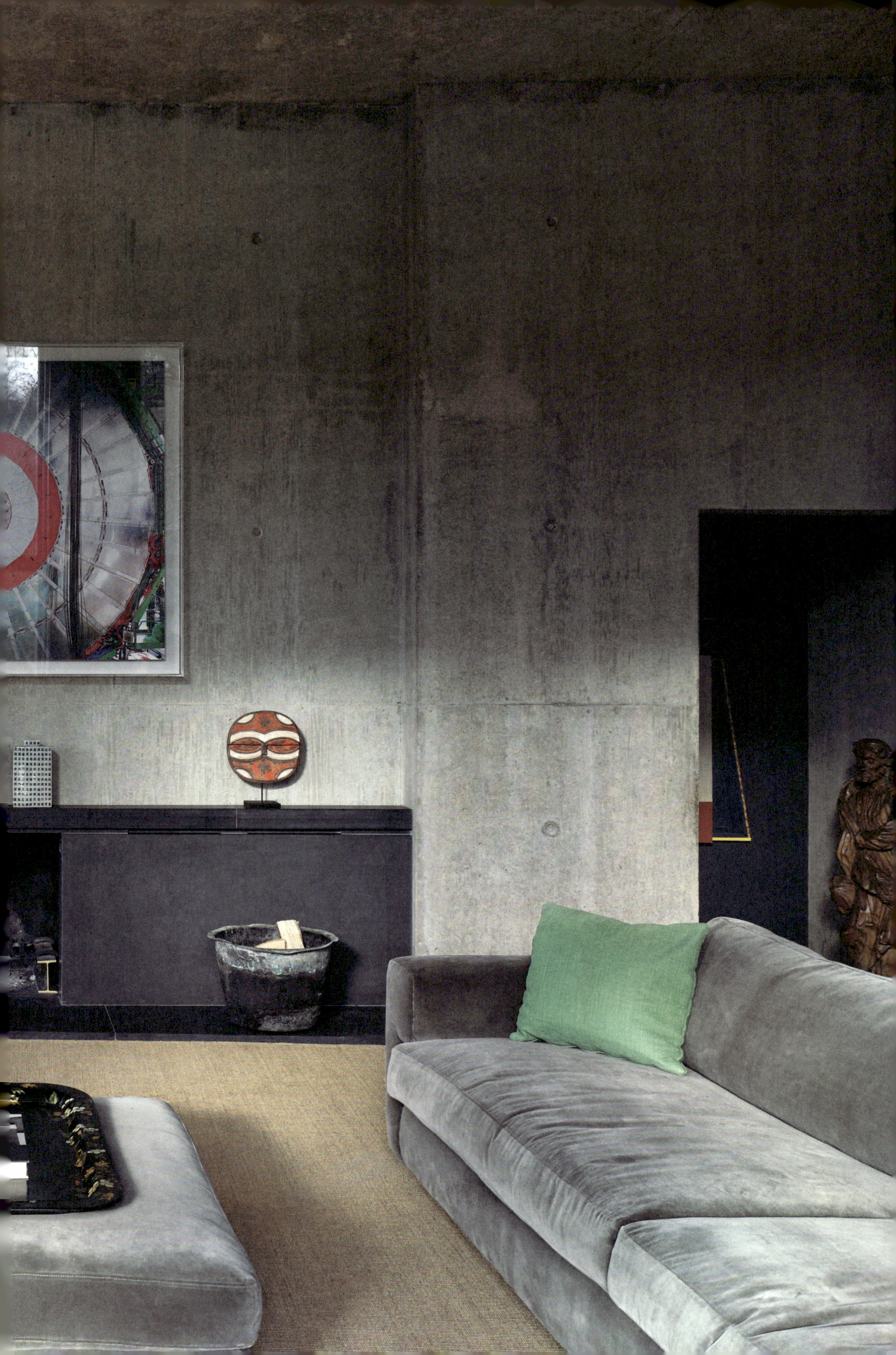

xv

xvii

xvi

xviii

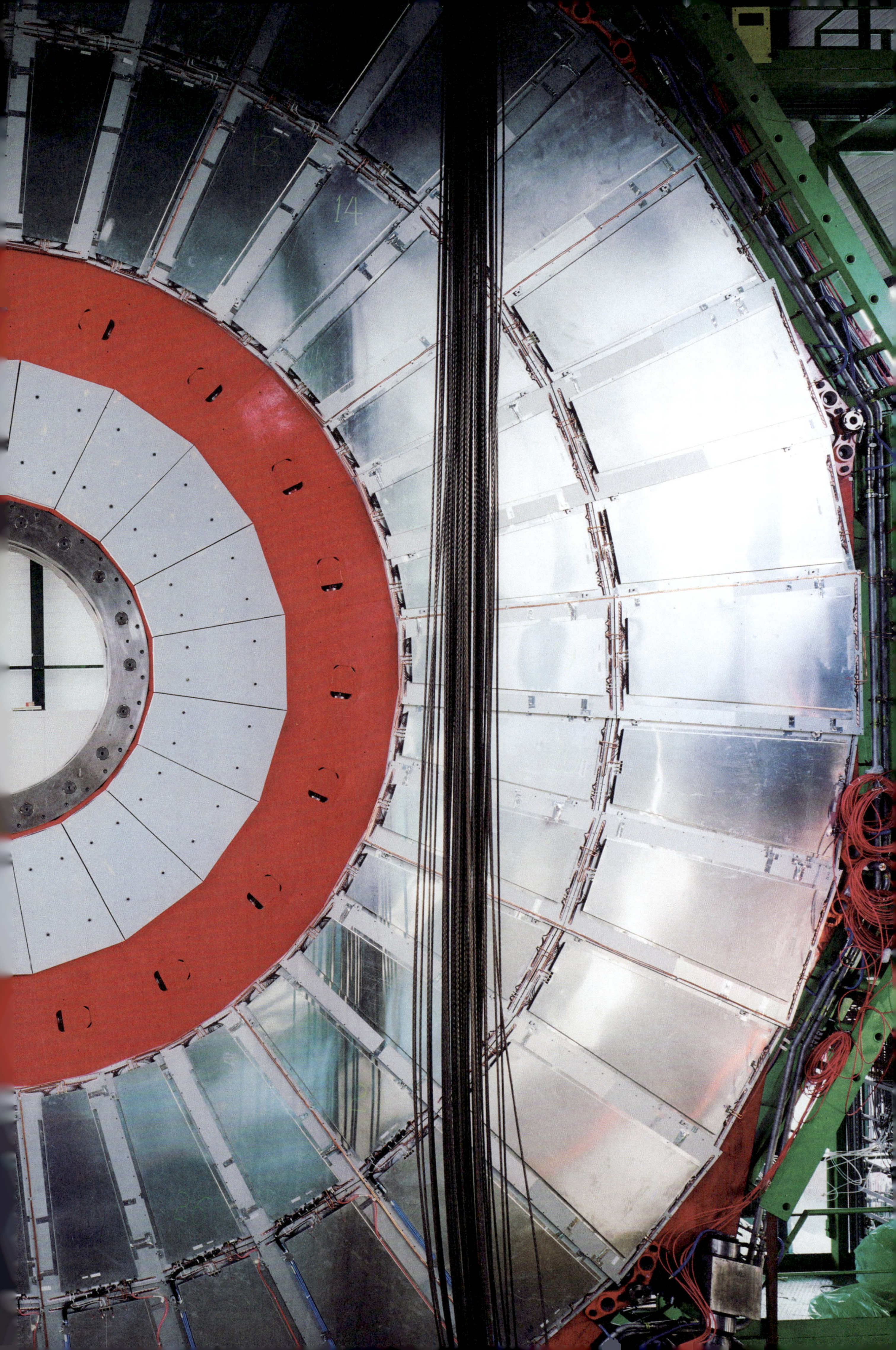
13
14

ZONE DOGS

PERCY, 2024

'All architecture is what you do to it when you look upon it,
(Did you think it was in the white or gray stone? or the lines of the arches and cornices?)' — WALT WHITMAN[1]

GEOFF DYER: A peculiarity of Andrei Tarkovsky's film *Stalker* is that although the 'Room' (where, it is claimed, one's deepest wish will come true) is in the 'Zone', it is not in a *House*. Strictly speaking, the Room is in some kind of building – we get glimpses of it as the three characters, Stalker, Writer and Professor, make their hesitant and meandering way towards it – but this house is never once mentioned or referred to. All the talk – of which there's a lot – is only and always about the Room, not the larger structure of which it is a part. It's as if this piece of synecdoche enables Tarkovsky to pose a philo-architectural question or thought experiment: can you have a Room without a House? Seen in this light, Adam Richards's house near Petworth builds on this lack, an attempt to contain or provide a dwelling for this houseless Room.

There is an appropriateness about this, since although one's very deepest desire – the thing that defines one – can lie so deeply embedded in one's being that one may be unconscious of it, as was tragically the case with Stalker's mentor, Porcupine, our longing for the ideal home lies at the next, more easily accessible level of consciousness. Contemplating an old photograph by Charles Clifford of a house in the Alhambra, Roland Barthes declares 'quite simply' in *Camera Lucida* (1980): 'I want to live there.' This desire affects him 'at a depth and according to roots' which he cannot understand. More broadly, looking at 'landscapes of predilection' like this, Barthes continues, 'it is as if I were certain of having been there or of going there'.[2] (The Zone might be described as the ultimate landscape of predilection, at the heart of which is the Room, which reveals one's deepest predilection.)

Expressing herself in a lighter style than Barthes, Meghan Daum gives voice to an ironic version of the same longing with her book entitled *Life Would Be Perfect If I Lived in That House* (2010). That's the dream, of course, that estate agents are always ready to pander to and exploit. The problem, unless you're unusually wealthy, is the way *that* house is always either wildly or tantalisingly beyond your financial grasp. Approaching the Room, you are on the threshold of the absolute; in the Room it's only your deepest wish that is realised and revealed. But when it comes to buying real-life rooms in actually existing houses, compromise is the name of the game. You scale down what you would ideally have to make it fit your budget. The good news is that the place you end up being able to afford can always be improved. Walls can be knocked down or, at the very least, painted over. If you do it yourself, an entire industry exists in order to make this ameliorative intention seem as painless and inexpensive as possible.

Unless something goes wrong or the funds set aside for the project turn out to be inadequate, it's likely that the place that wasn't quite the place of your dreams will look better – or at least more to your taste – within a year of purchase than it did when you first saw it and resigned yourself to the fact that it was within your price range. But time does not stop at this weightless moment of maximised home improvement and satisfaction. Over time your home becomes, in Philip Larkin's well-known expression of domestic resignation, 'A joyous shot at how things ought to be, /Long fallen wide'.[3] Your deepest desire, eventually, is to slump into the sofa, not to spend any more effort or money on trying to perfect the room in which this sofa – which could itself do with reupholstering or, ideally, replacing – happens to be.

At one point, after his two 'clients' have both, for different reasons, expressed their indifference or hostility to the Room, Stalker contemplates moving into the Zone with his wife and their daughter, Monkey. It's a logical enough plan. After all, the first words he uttered when he got to this colourful place with Writer and Professor were, 'Here we are, home at last!' So, yes, why not make a home in the place you call home? Well, from a real estate point of view there are advantages and disadvantages. First, there's the location. The Zone is by definition inaccessible to conventional forms of transport. Getting there is a right old palaver and even if you make it in one piece – evading the border guards, sneaking in across the frontier and so forth – there is the further complication that although the distance to the Room is not great you have to take a radically circuitous, testing and constantly changing route to get there. Pressed for more specific information on exactly how long it takes and how far it is, the honest estate agent can only reply, 'I'm afraid, it's impossible to say.'

There is some wildlife that could presumably be caught and cooked but there are no shops, cafes or bars like the one Stalker, Professor and Writer start out from and end up back in. (*How* they get back there is never made clear; it's possible that, by some fluke of rail connections or whatever, the journey back to 'civilisation' is nothing like so perilous as was the journey into the Zone.) Another positive is that there are very few competing buyers. You're unlikely to get gazumped because, as the despairing Stalker tells his wife, no one except him gives a toss about the stupid Zone. On the downside – it seems more appropriate to mingle the positives and negatives in this way when discussing a place which changes, from appearing magical to entirely ordinary and back, moment by moment – the lack of schools might be something to consider (though Stalker has 'home-schooling fanatic' written all over him). As is the fact that the Room is a classic example of what American realtors call a do-up. Nothing works – except the phone, strangely – and everything is in need of repair: floors, ceiling, plumbing, lights, you name it. Everything man-made is in the process of being reclaimed by nature. Damp – rising, falling, sideways creeping – is a major concern. When Frank Lloyd Wright's clients complained that their roof was leaking, he replied 'That's how you can tell it's a roof', and it's only by this contrarian definition that the roof of the Room can be viewed as fit for any kind of purpose. (What would happen if some punter got there whose deepest desire was for a roof that never leaked?) On a positive note again, planning permission is unlikely to be an issue, or at least planning restrictions are not going to be strictly policed or enforced.

All of which is background to my visit to Adam's house on a beautifully inappropriate day in June 2022: blue sky, bright sun, temperature in the high 70s. The journey was also a reversal of the originating trip in *Stalker* in that I set out from Zone 2 of the London transport network and sped through 3, 4, 5 and 6 into the Zoneless world of Woking and beyond. Summer in England, that blighted Jerusalem of discontent, staff shortages and the latest in a series of Covid surges, but still with enough greenery and pubs to keep alive the dream of Albion on which the appeal of Brexit depended and from which it is still in the process of waking. If I'd come a day later, I wouldn't have come at all. The biggest rail strike in 30 years was due to start the next day, the first in a planned season of disputes that would inflict fresh wounds on the injury-prone body politic. Nice trees, though, and fields beyond the tight lanes, verdant in that distinctly English way (that always makes me think, strangely, not of English films but of the trees and meadows in *Mirror*, the film Tarkovsky made before *Stalker*).

The house, looking distinctly new, sits in a low valley as if waiting for time to soften that newness and make it look a part of the landscape rather than an addition to – an imposition on – it. (Fifty years from now it will have merged softly into its surroundings.) This sense is exacerbated by the house's impregnability. There is no door to be seen as you approach, no way in. Instead, the drive slopes down to the house and winds around it. Nothing if not discreet, the entrance is hidden round the back of the house: a small grey door marked by a spectacular lack of splendour. It looks like the negative equivalent of an emergency exit: an emergency entrance to be used only if the official (in this case, non-existent) one might, for whatever reason, be faulty. This extreme compression emphasises the scale of the main room one ... I was going to say 'enters' but it's perhaps more evocative to say *burrows* up into: an epic kitchen-cum-everything room with what looks like a mightily enlarged pew separating it from a kids' play area. One's sense of scale is further emphasised by a false perspective: the side walls are not parallel but converge slightly in the distance, with floorboards emerging at right angles from each of these tapering walls and meeting in the centre at a slight diagonal, further enhancing the perspectival illusion. Undeniably striking it may be, but this is not the kind of room where you could waste an evening passively. It's an *active* room. So it's a relief to leave here and find oneself, via some steps and another little passage twisting off slightly to the left, in something that has leisurely elements of a traditional Home Counties drawing room. There are sofas (of the sort that we dreamed of upgrading to several paragraphs back), tables with books, 'great windows open to the south', in Yeats's phrase (even if the direction, in this instance, is actually north, west or east). Beyond the windows is a green extent of lawn that continues the perspectival beckoning of the previous room. About *this* room, there's something satisfyingly weird: the result of a combination of the austere concrete and the faded, old tapestries completely covering one wall (and partially covered, in turn, by modern artworks). There's a turntable, albums stacked up, ready to be heard, and books to be seen, picked up, read.

Upstairs there are two floors of bedrooms and guest rooms. The views from high, up here, emphasise the loveliness of the spot: the clipped green of the lawn, the longer grass of fields and, beyond that, the trees and rolling hills. Against the green, like an animate shadow, comes a perfect black dog, big-eyed and thin, moving at a fraction of the speed of which he's capable. There are *Stalker*-ish touches throughout the house – all carefully plotted and planned – but it was this dog, Percy, that did it for me: a jet-black Lurcher, with that look of quivering and patient intelligence that seems, also, like a manifestation of mutually needed love. At one point the arrival of gardeners provoked a bark or two but they're the quietest of dogs, lurchers, so that they seem a pure presence, a pure manifestation of the idea of themselves. You'd hear the faintest scratch of paws on the carpet and then this lovely lithe black shape, a three-dimensional silhouette, would shimmy across the room and curl up on the sofa for a few moments. Everything else was arranged; Percy, being a creature, brought that necessary element of the unplanned and unpredictable. This too may have been planned. In the Zone the three travellers come across a dog – a German Shepherd, I think. When we see them back in the bar, the dog is there with them: living proof that they have been to the Zone. As Stalker, his wife and Monkey head home, the dog is with them. So Percy – thinner, even blacker – perhaps serves a similar function: a sentient reminder that it is possible not only for your deepest wish to be granted but also that this desire (for the perfect house) can be actively achieved, designed, built – and lived in. He comes and goes, this Zone dog, but, like the room in the house he pads through so quietly, he is here to stay.

1 'A Song For Occupations', in Walt Whitman, *Leaves of Grass*, 1885.
2 Roland Barthes, *Camera Lucida*, Hill and Wang, New York, 1981.
3 'Home Is So Sad', in Philip Larkin, *The Whitsun Weddings*, 1964.

xix

xx

xxii

xxi

xxiii

xxiv

83

A REPOSITORY FOR FRAGMENTS

REF	OBJECT	PAGE
i	Robert Mangold (American b.1937):	
	Multiple panel paintings 1973–6; A book of silkscreen prints, 1992	14
ii	Adam Richards (British b.1967):	
	Nithurst Model, bronze and wood, 2022	15
iii	Still from Andrei Tarkovsky's *Stalker*, 1979	26
iv	Artist unknown: Italian sculpted figure, wood, 16th/17th century	27
v	Ronan & Erwan Bouroullec (French b.1971, b.1976):	
	Clouds, wool-coated fabric, 2009	28–9
vi	HelenA Pritchard (South African b.1975):	
	Aperture Painting, insect vinyl mesh on two found wood panels; oil paint, household paints, gloss paint, pigment on found velvet fabric, 2017	30-1
vii	Artist unknown: Mexican sculpted figures, wood, possibly 18th century	33
viii	Keith Wilson (British b.1965):	
	Untitled, photograph on gloss paper, 2004	48–9
ix	Artist unknown: *The Lachesis, or fatal Viper*, coloured print, 1801	50
x	Robert Mangold (American b.1937):	
	Multiple panel paintings 1973–6; A book of silkscreen prints, 1992	54–5
xi	HelenA Pritchard (South African b.1975):	
	Aperture Painting, construction vinyl mesh, gesso, oil paint, polyvinyl on linen, 2018	56
xii	Designer unknown: Cordeaux insulators, glazed porcelain, 20th century	57
xiii	Artist unknown: Italian carved wood painted Madonna and Child, 17th/18th century	60
xiv	Designer unknown: Metal circus letters, 19th/20th century	61
xv	HelenA Pritchard (South African b.1975):	
	Unit 17, construction, gesso, oil paint, polyvinyl on linen, 2018	68
xvi	Designer unknown: Porcelain pots, China, unknown date	69
xvii	Artist unknown: Teke Kidumu mask, Congo, wood and pigment, unknown date	69
xviii	Simon Norfolk (Nigerian/British b.1963):	
	Untitled (Large Hadron Collider No. 2), C-type print, 2007	70–1
xix	Artist unknown: Bwa sun mask, Burkina Faso, wood and pigment, unknown date	78
xx	Jos de Mey (Belgian 1928–2007):	
	Struktuurraster, screenprint, 1973	79
xxi	Le Corbusier (Swiss 1887–1965):	
	Original lithograph from the portfolio *Entre-deux*, plate 4 of 17, 1957–64. Edition of 250. Published by Editions Forces-vives, Paris.	80
xxii	Artist unknown: Wrestler's ex-voto, Mexico, 20th century	80
xxiii	Artist unknown: European sculpted head of a saint, Portugal, wood, 17th century	81
xxiv	Claire Pestaille (British b.1975):	
	The Witches After Party, oil on canvas, 2004	82–3
xxv	Artist unknown: sculpted stone head, origin unknown	90
xxvi	Artist unknown: *Phenomena of the Moon*, coloured print, 1798	91
xxvii	Artist unknown: European sculpted figure of Saint Bartholomew, wood, late 17th/ early 18th century	94
xxviii	Dame Elisabeth Frink (British 1930–93):	
	The Pardoner's Tale from the series *The Canterbury Tales*, etching with aquatint on paper, 1972	95
xxix	Bruce McLean (British b.1944):	
	Study for Carnival Canteen Door Painting, collage and mixed media, 1994	98–9
xxx	Jane Edden (British b.1966):	
	125 Hawker Siddley G-AVGW from the series *Flying Jackets*, resin and pheasant feathers in Perspex case, 2013	122

CORINNA DEAN: Encountering the Russian author Vladimir Nabokov's words in his sci-fi novella *Lance* (1952), 'the future is but the obsolete in reverse',[1] one is forced to recalibrate linear thought and scramble our ordering of things. This undoing of time is what the director Andrei Tarkovsky in his 1979 screen film *Stalker* delights in. The film's narrative suggests a positioning outside of time, hinting at a near future in which the earth has been wounded through an undisclosed environmental catastrophe; the infected ecology runs invisibly but threateningly through the film's landscapes. I interpret the quest into the 'Zone' to seek the 'Room' – a forbidden site which acts as the fourth protagonist in *Stalker*, lying amongst the ruins of an industrial behemoth – as the failure of Modernism's Promethean dream of a technological fix: here nature is polluted and pollutes. And it is within this framing that we can view Adam Richards's architectural composition, Nithurst, and its accompanying collection of objects.

To call Nithurst a house or villa does it a disservice; instead it reads as an object which acknowledges time as a tool that can be sculpted with. The architect is both reserved and orchestral, adopting a role which arranges the pieces of the building's form, spaces and materials, but also the objects within. This combination of house and objects creates a powerful and unique architectural proposition, which draws you in, but not through grand gestures. The pocket entrance hall, for instance, surprises with its demureness; a heavy scent of resin lingers from a stack of freshly sawn firewood, reminding one not to rely too fully on retinal perception.

Released from the entrance chamber one arrives at the main living space, comprising kitchen, dining room and children's playroom. The window apertures sit above eye level, directing the focus on what it means to exist as a family within a dwelling. This main living space evokes Tarkovsky's church-like antechamber to the Room in *Stalker*, its floor consisting of rippling dunes, and with distant light from above. This is the setting for a key scene in the film where the tension between faith and doubt is brought to a head.

SEE PAGE 26

Nithurst is a repository for fragments that interplay with the architecture. These are not just props, augmenting the narrative 'reading' of the building, but have the effect of intensifying our emotional responses to the spaces. Adam seeks out objects, effigies, sculptures and paintings – many rich with a scientific trope undercut by a more human subtext – demonstrating a precarity of life as we straddle between the rational and spiritual, a quest to make sense of our material lives. A painted wooden sculpture standing on the kitchen counter, carried back from Mexico, depicts an archangel put through a Gaudiesque carnival interpretation.

33

30-1   This piece sits in dialogue with a large painting, set out as a diptych, by the artist HelenA Pritchard that references the work of renowned twentieth-century abstract artists. Pritchard's painting is a riff on Rothko, making a gentle poke at the revered genius of the master with her introduction of stitched repairs to the canvas and found roadside materials. The dialogue between these works and the space seems analogous to the themes of faith and doubt that Tarkovsky explores.

28-9   A hanging textile titled *Clouds*, by the French designers Ronan & Erwan Bouroullec, hovers above the portal through which one departs this main space, leading towards the sitting room. Constructed from sculptural faceted fabric tiles assembled with silicone bands, the pieces can be arranged according to the wishes of the installer. Here, they have been composed to suggest a kind of 'fractal sky' – a representation of the heavens positioned where a reredos would be placed in a church. However, in place of an altar is the doorway to a passage leading to the sitting room. Dominating the view through this portal is an artwork by Keith

48–9   Wilson: a large black-and-white photograph of a particle accelerator; the enormity of the scientific subject matter provides a suitable punctuation point from which to counter the biblical tenets more concerned with ideas of transcendence that are held within the religious imagery described above.

Stalker shifts between black-and-white and colour, emphasising the contrast between the 'Zone' and the world beyond. Back to back with the Keith Wilson black-and-white image, and emphasising the transition from hall to sitting room, is a second image of a particle accelerator:

70-1   a photograph by Simon Norfolk of the Large Hadron Collider under construction, this time in full colour. Positioned above the fireplace on the centre line of the house, this image faces due south along the axis of the linear garden, which provides a painterly green line towards the midday sun. The relational aspect of these objects suggests a re-enactment of medieval cosmological diagrams, highlighting the theme of contrasting ideas of transcendence. This space is both uplifting and calming. A series

54-5   of prints by the American Minimalist artist Robert Mangold hangs against a collage of floor-to-ceiling seventeenth- and eighteenth-century tapestries. At first encounter Mangold's geometrical works look ordered, a display of mathematical formalism, but the subtle interruptions in the forms reveal an undoing of this presupposed order. It is this disruption which Adam would like you to infer through his work.

If Nithurst's sitting room is Richards's version of Tarkovsky's 'Room', then it has its own representation of the Stalker, in the form of a medieval

81   wooden head of a saint, suffering etched on its face. Other fragments –

ceramic electrical insulators, an animal skull etc. – act as reminders of the objects immersed in the stream of water into which the Stalker, exhausted, lays down to sleep.

57

Here, one is left to contemplate the disruptions of time as represented through the concept of the ruin. Whilst Tarkovsky had the tools of cinematography to create with, emphasising the play of light and dark, Richards has a different set of tools, dealing with the shaping of materials. The external brick walls provide a thick skin with a series of arches, stepping up to a three-storey tower. The deep reveals expose an inner core of barefaced in situ concrete, with all the imperfections that marked the surfaces during the pouring process, as well as water stains – intentionally left to reveal concrete's uneasy relationship to its technological primacy in solving a raft of social ills in early Modernism, before it slipped into a style. The striking, almost schizophrenic element of the brick outer wall, in dialogue with the concrete inner layer, reveals Nithurst's dystopian aspect; the fragility of the orchestration of objects, landscape, sun path and space is a careful balance, but one able to throw our own subjectivity out of kilter.

Returning from the arcadian setting of the sitting room, the stair passage is presided over by an ecclesiastical sculpture of St Bartholomew, ghoulishly carrying his own skin over one shoulder. This reminder of the corporeal clash of theology and the material sets the scene for the experience of the staircase, where wall-hung objects highlight the more physical/animal side of man: images of animals (horses, dogs, a serpent) are juxtaposed with an African 'sun' mask from the Bwa people of Burkina Faso. The route to the upper floors is serpentine, including a minstrel-esque gallery, which offers views back onto the main space.

94

50, 93

78

On ascending to the final floor, the single run staircase on axis takes its reference from Michael Powell and Emeric Pressburger's 1946 film *A Matter of Life and Death*, where the protagonist, a Second World War RAF pilot, hovers indecisively between two worlds. A small birdlike sculpture encased in Perspex, titled *125 Hawker Siddley G-AVGW*, from the artist Jane Edden's *Flying Jackets* series, is installed, marking the arrival at the final step, a small memento mori of Adam's father, a pilot who died in a plane crash when Adam was a baby. The jacket is the size of a hummingbird and was created from hundreds of feathers to produce a piece that inhabits a hybrid space between avian and human.

122

From the third floor one can scan the surrounding landscape, elevated above the tree canopy. Here, Adam describes the inspiration of a watercolour by the British artist Paul Nash, *Mansions of the Dead* (1932). This work depicts birdlike forms inhabiting strange, grid-like structures in the sky.

109

Adam says the grid of grey bricks on the south facade of the house was inspired by this image, and here on the top floor we are framed by that grid (standing alongside the Jane Edden piece), our future deaths prefigured. Nash's combined work as a landscape painter and war artist developed a landscape vocabulary far removed from the bucolic or the picturesque, the latter heightened through the fashion of viewing landscapes through a concave handheld mirror called a 'Claude glass', which involved turning one's back on the real landscape and gazing upon its framed reflection. Nash's war paintings remind one of the ability of destruction to disrupt our somewhat conditioned aesthetic frameworks of nature and culture.

The promenade through Nithurst resonates with the words of Nabokov, sitting playfully alongside our investment in the material and the ability of the ruin to romanticise the past and respond to shifting time frames. Adam's introduction of the idea of the ruin demonstrates a curiosity in conceptualising the unfinished, which leaves the building open to its future orientation, as in the case of *Stalker*, a successional landscape of resilient ecologies which takes hold of the Zone. Perhaps pre-empting this, Adam has created his own contemporary ruin onto which narratives around the moving and still life can be played out.

Reflecting on Nithurst, the architecture appears to dance between overlapping spatial narratives heightened and punctuated by objects, paintings, sculptural pieces and *objets trouvés*, all intended to either distil or provoke a sense of engagement with the space. The house becomes a framework onto which different scenarios can be projected, all ultimately reminding us of our vulnerability in relation to divergent temporal zones – immediate, geological and cosmological.

1   Vladimir Nabokov, *Lance*, 1952, first published in *The New Yorker*.

XXV

ASTRONOMY. Plate IV.

Fig 1.

Phenomena of the Moon.

London Published as the Act directs May 12, 1798 by J.Wilkes.

J.Pass sculp

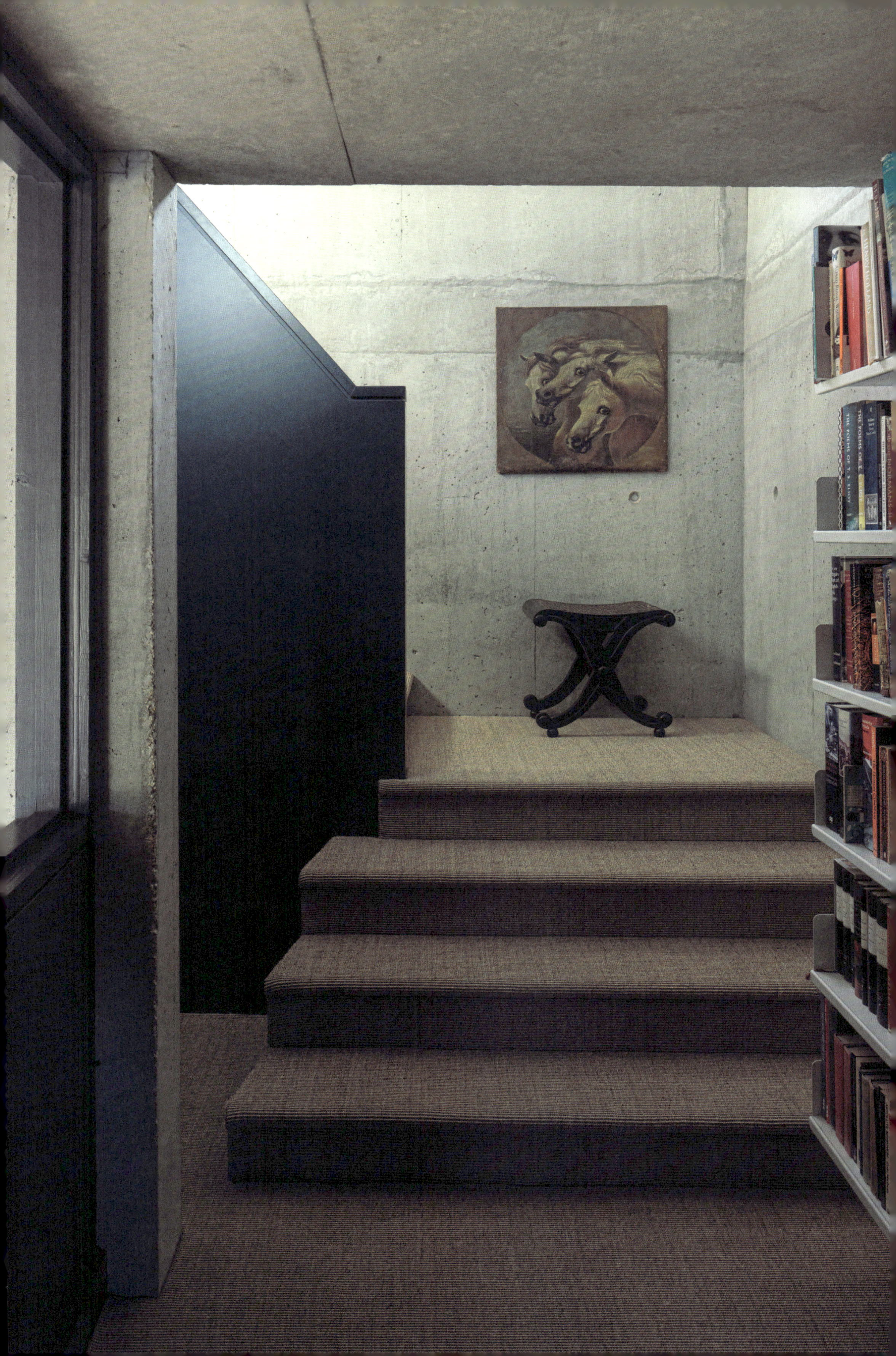

xxvii

xxviii

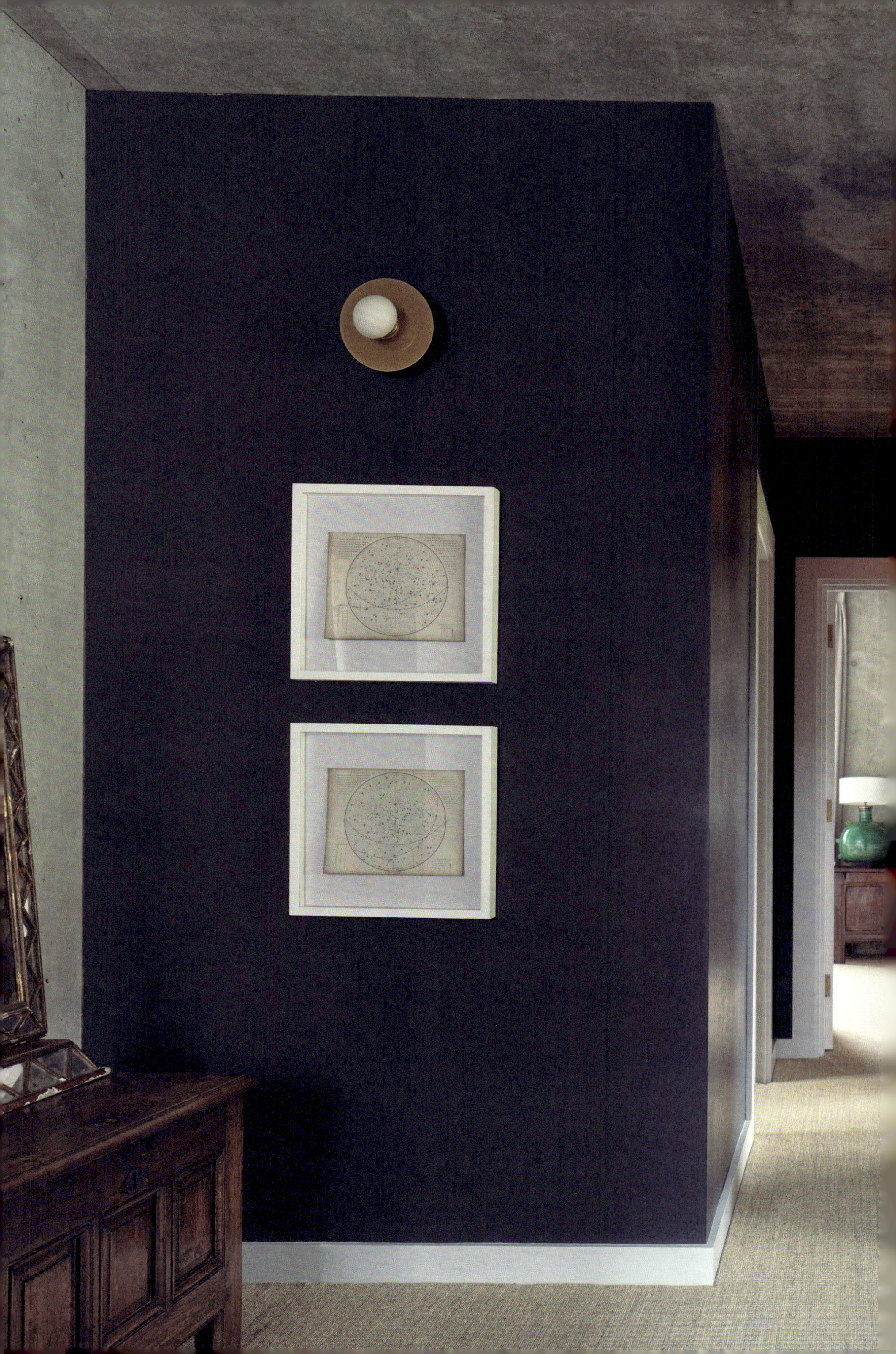

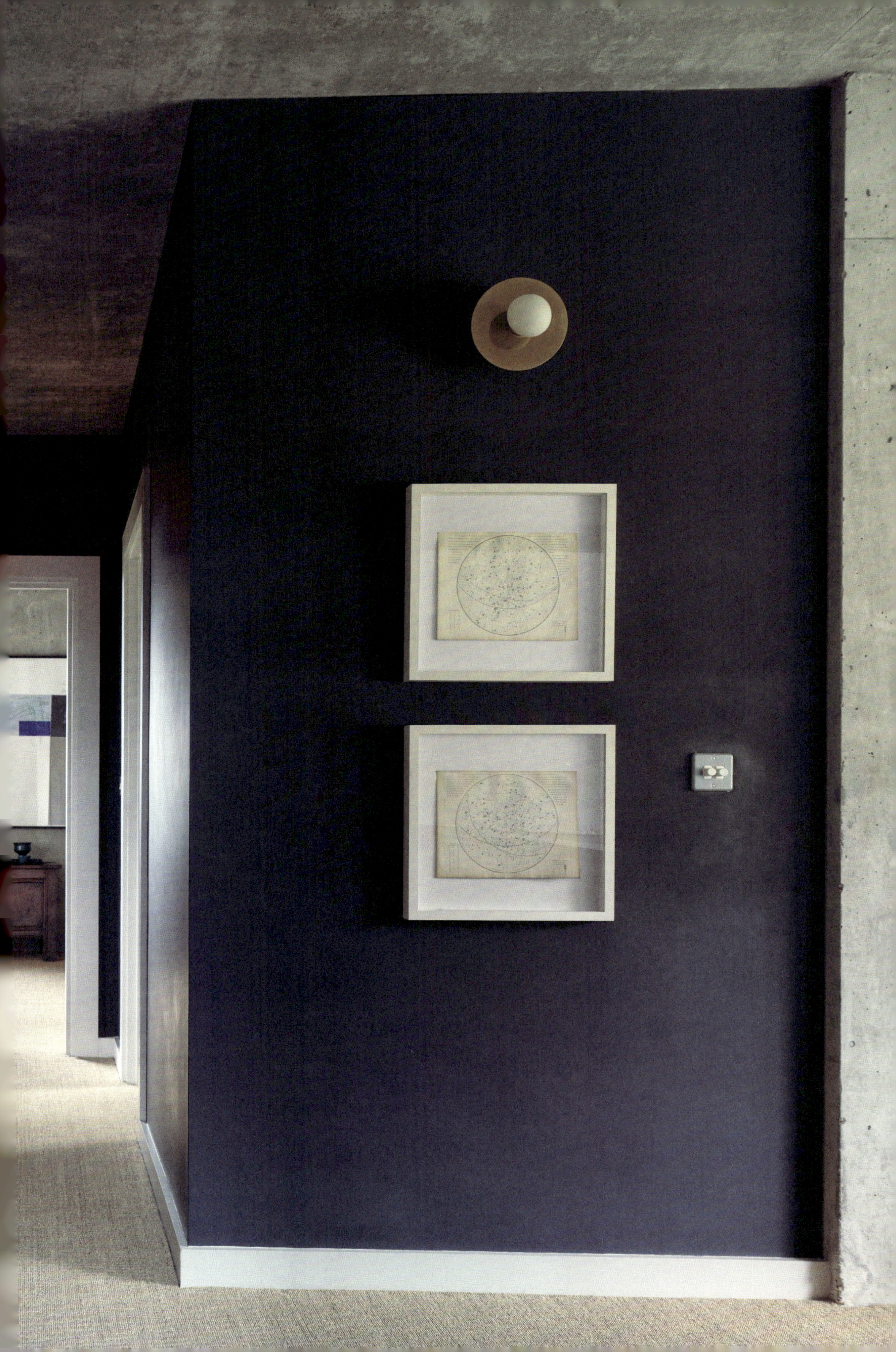

Study for Carnival
Door Painting

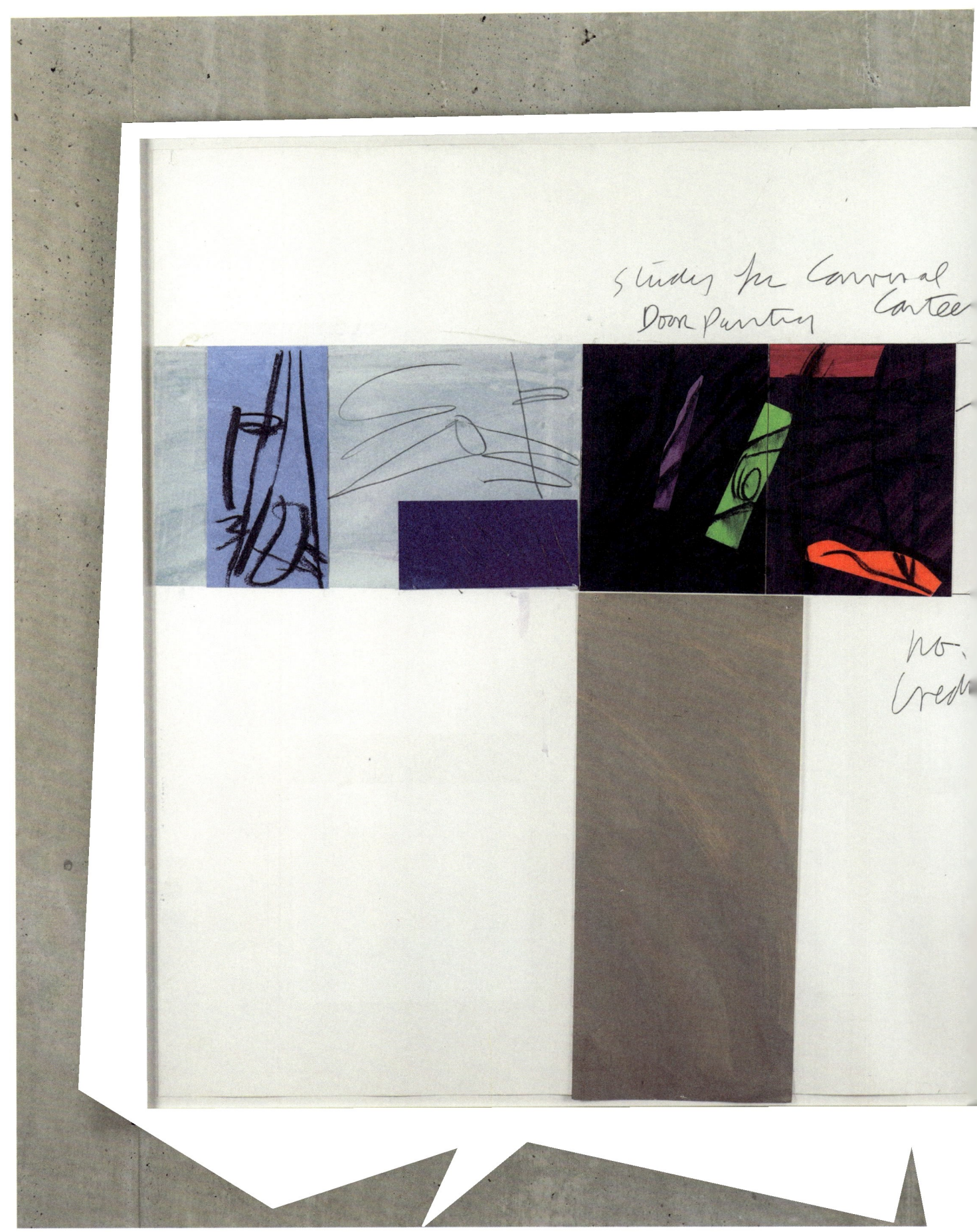

xxix

stark walls

POINTS OF REFERENCE – IV

TAKERO SHIMAZAKI: The adventurous route up to the sleeping areas is like climbing to the loft spaces in Palladio's villas. As in Palladian stairs, one is granted a breather on the mezzanine level with a window overlooking the main room. Having negotiated the tight, dark staircase, the view of the main room from above is majestic; the clarity of its plan, like a meticulous stage set, makes 'looking back' both rewarding and thought-provoking.

The journey continues towards the bedrooms on the first and second floors. Two incorporate private maze-like stairs that take you down to en-suite bathrooms at the mezzanine level. This is at first very disorienting and it's hard to figure out what is happening in terms of the levels. Here one appreciates the smart use of the towers in the main room, with both en-suites encapsulated within them, thereby freeing up floor area in the bedrooms.

Rising from the first floor is a tapering central staircase whose design refers to the 'stairway to heaven' in Michael Powell and Emeric Pressburger's 1946 film *A Matter of Life and Death* – about an airman ascending to the afterlife – and so, indirectly, to Richards's pilot father. At the second floor, you are greeted by vast windows facing the south landscape. Paired main bedrooms are arranged with dressing areas and a central bathroom at the opposite end. Here, again, absolutely everything is laid out symmetrically. The central steps to the shower cubicle from the open bathroom area are particularly impressive, elevating this daily routine into an architectural ritual.

MICHAEL POWELL AND EMERIC PRESSBURGER,
STILL FROM *A MATTER OF LIFE AND DEATH*, 1946

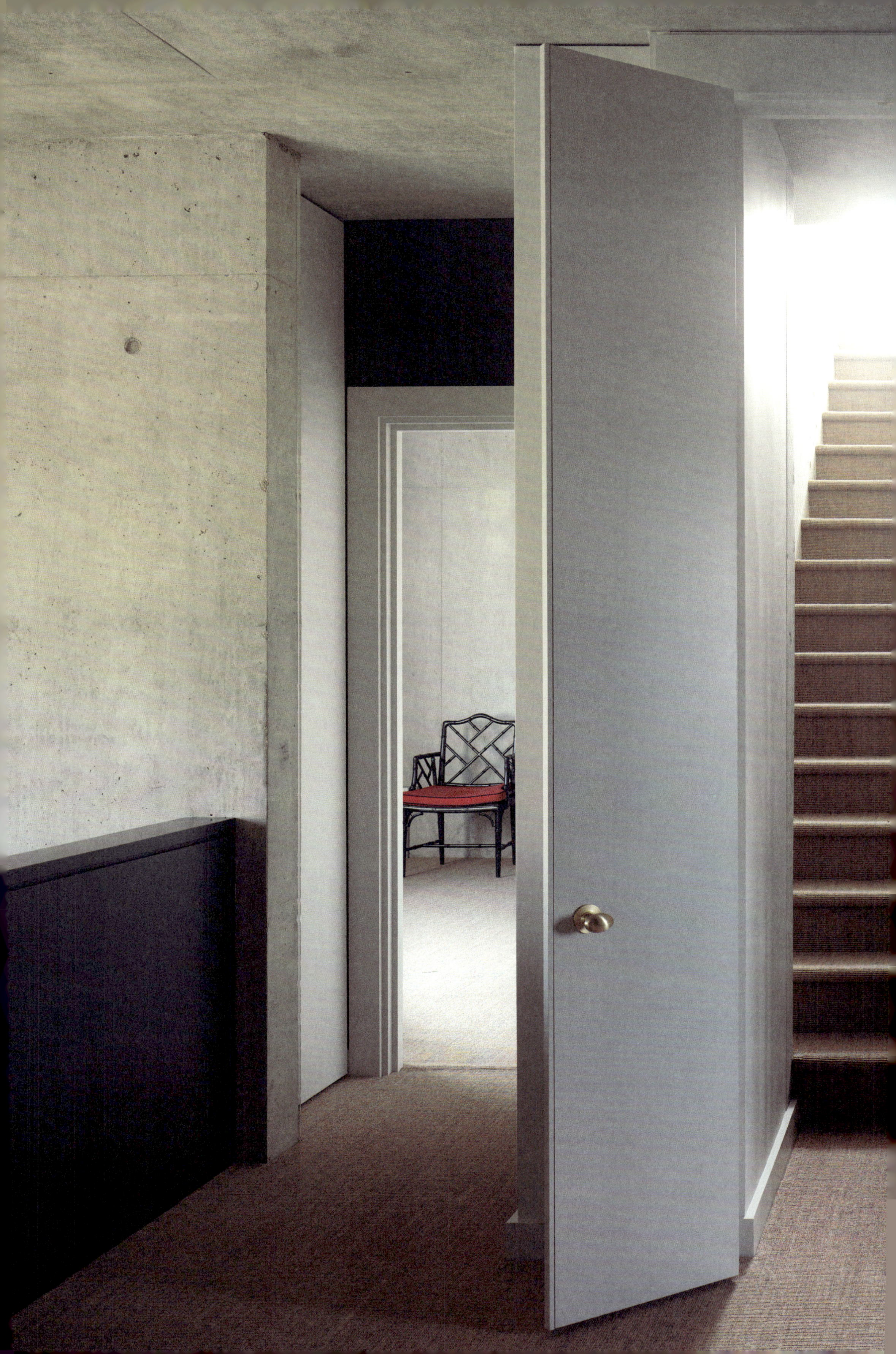

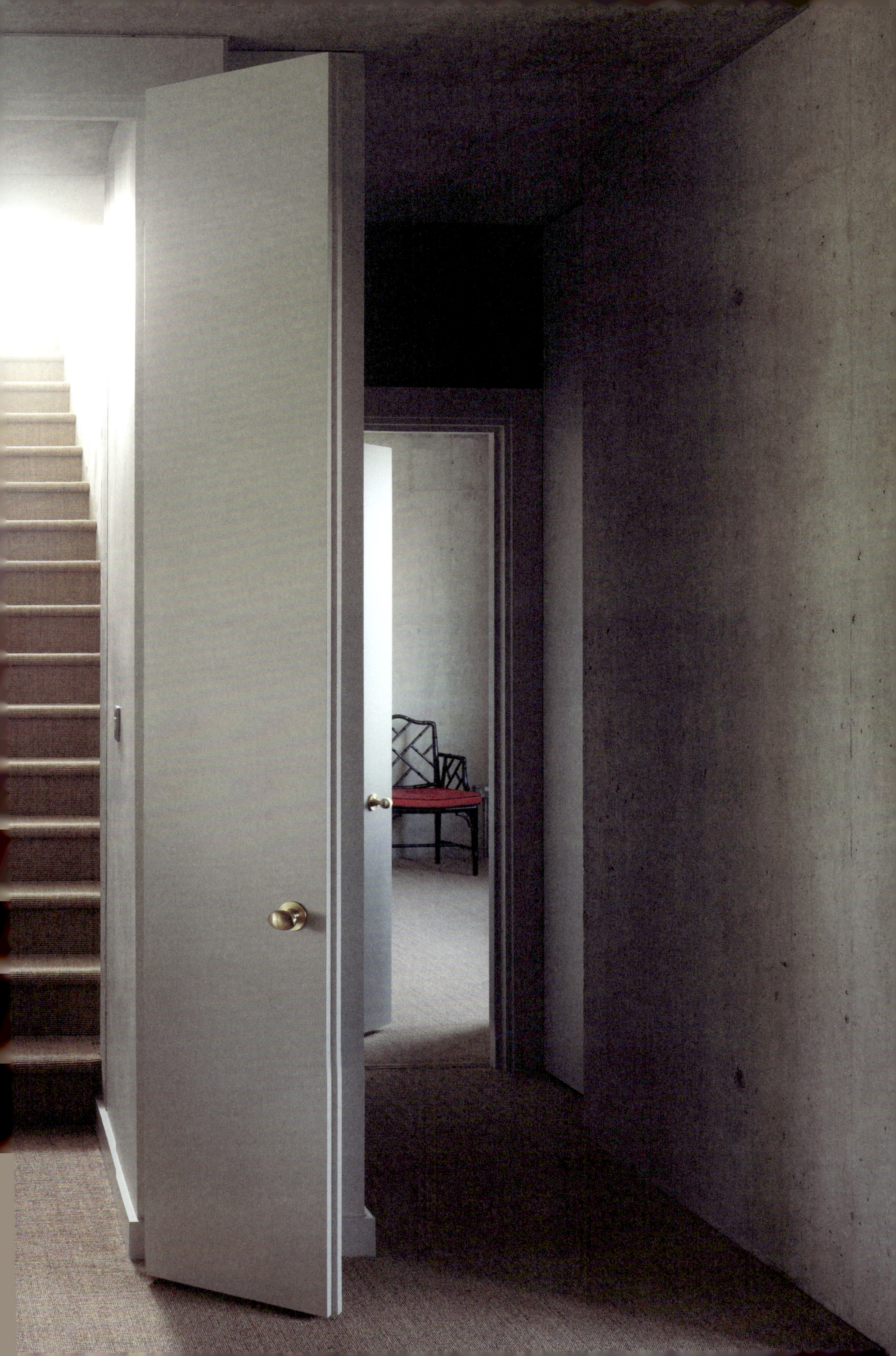

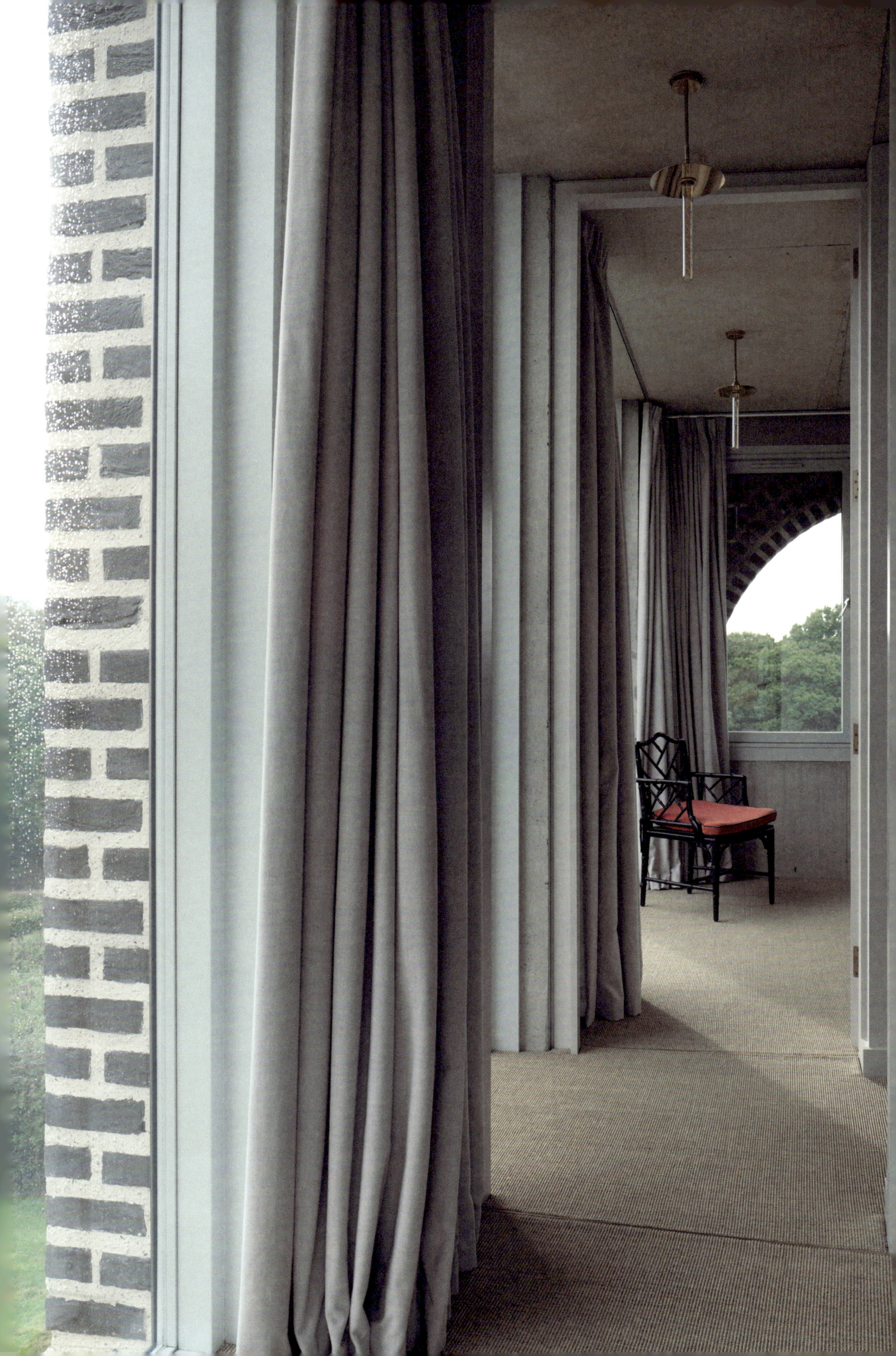

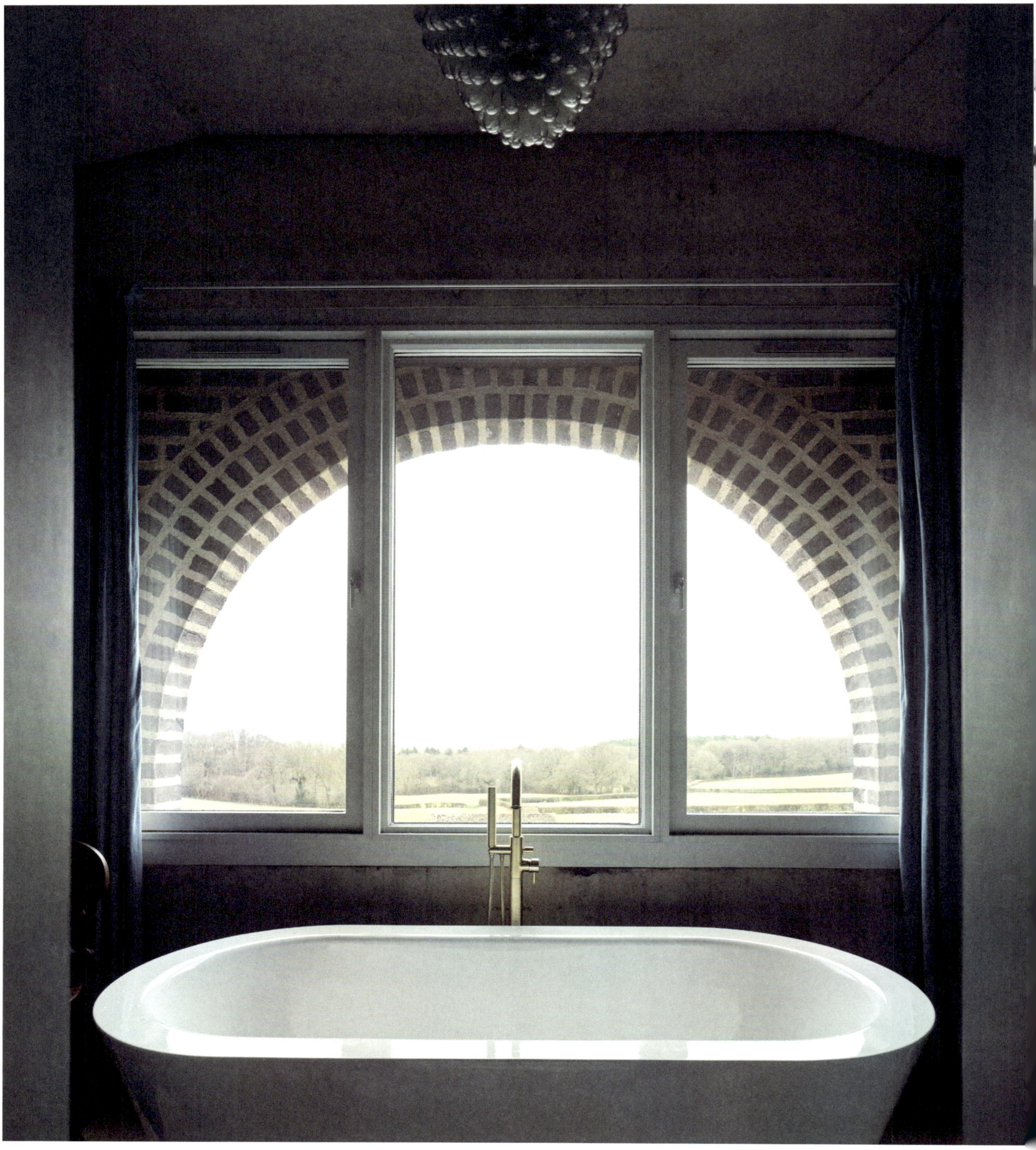

VANISHING POINT

PAUL NASH, *MANSIONS OF THE DEAD*, 1932

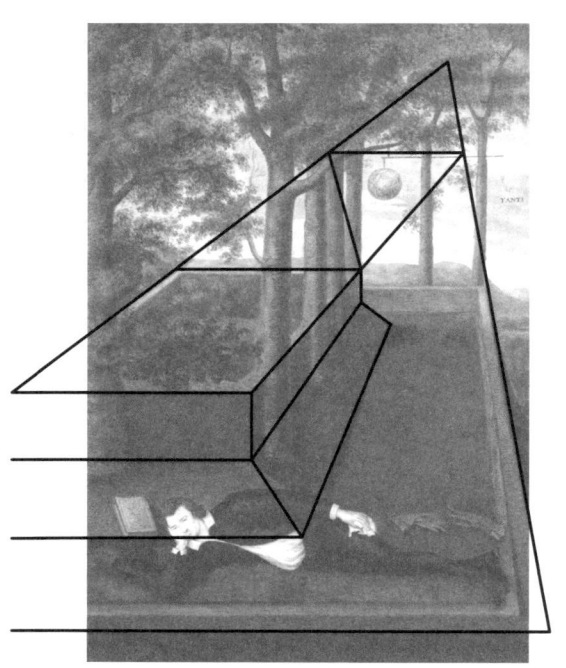

PERSPECTIVE OVERLAY OF NICHOLAS HILLIARD, *PORTRAIT OF HENRY PERCY*, 1590–95

'Tarkovsky's films are about the perpetual search for home, the lost home of childhood ... The conflict and dialectics between the notions of "architecture" and "home" are also a central concern for architects.'
—JUHANI PALLASMAA[1]

STOP[2]

ADAM RICHARDS: Of course we all stop in the end. It's the one thing of which we can be sure amongst the tumult of our lives in the world. Perhaps it is this knowledge that drives us to seek a state-of-being that transcends both conditions. This search can be a kind of quest, or journey, and is often bound up with ideas of place, highlighting a human need to find laws, or patterns or meaning in our environment. At Nithurst, the use of optical illusion, materials and cultural fragments underlines the psychological nature of the 'journey' implicit within the house.

Deep in a hidden valley, the buildings at Nithurst rise from farmed fields, won from the woods in the late Saxon period. Old maps, and ridges and ditches in the woods, attest to a landscape changing subtly over long periods, with the boundary between pasture and woodland ebbing and flowing. One such change took place at the end of the sixteenth century, as the result of an unequal power struggle that saw the then Nithurst farmer, William James,[3] pitted against local landowner Henry Percy, 9th Earl of Northumberland.[4] One of the country's most powerful figures, Percy had taken over local farm tenants' land in order to increase the size of his deer park at Petworth House. In a remarkable case, the tenants fought back, led by the charismatic William James. Inevitably, the earl eventually prevailed, but had to resort to bribery and intimidation to do so.

This contested landscape can be seen in Nicholas Hilliard's 1590s cabinet miniature depicting Henry Percy. Known as the 'Wizard Earl' because of his scientific and alchemical interests, Percy is shown lying in a hilltop garden on his Petworth estate, presumably on the land enclosed from his tenants. In the background can be glimpsed William James's farmland at Nithurst. This image – an *impresa*[5] – contains hidden meanings: the image of an ethereal sphere balanced by a feather and the word '*TANTI*' hangs from a tree in a formal garden. The painting's meaning has been subject to much speculative interpretation, particularly in relation to hermeticism and alchemy. The strange perspective lines of the rectilinear hedges invite us to trace their vanishing point – and in doing so we discover that a version of an alchemical symbol lies hidden in the image, surrounding the moon-like sphere,[6] and hovering over the landscape where Nithurst has now been built.

If alchemy was interpreted by Percy and his circle as a metaphor for an inner, 'spiritual' quest,[7] then Hilliard's imposition of an arcane perspectival geometry over the contested landscape at Nithurst suggests a relationship between inner journey and actual place. This relationship between an inner journey and a quest through a contested landscape is also present in Andrei Tarkovsky's 1979 film, *Stalker*. Two seemingly allegorical figures, Writer and Professor, hire the Stalker to lead them into the 'Zone' – a forbidden region, where an alien visitation seems to have resulted in the suspension of the normal rules of physics, and a sense that the landscape itself is somehow sentient, and potentially malevolent. At the heart of the Zone is a 'Room', capable – it is rumoured – of granting the deepest wishes of those who enter it. Tarkovsky's film follows the protagonists' quest to reach this Room. Hilliard's hidden geometry has an echo in the navigational method used by the Stalker as they cross the Zone: he throws strips of fabric tied to metal nuts in zigzagging lines to see if the way ahead is safe.

As they progress through the Zone, Tarkovsky's characters' motivations for reaching the Room come in and out of focus. Meanwhile, the Stalker's faith in the power of the Zone is confronted by the doubts of his clients, all of which comes to a head in a key scene in a vast, chapel-like concrete antechamber to the Room. Here the power of the Zone is seemingly revealed, and viewers can perhaps understand the Zone to be Tarkovsky's version of a pre-enlightenment world, animated by magic and superstition. However, there is a blurring of geography and psychology; like a grail-quest it is also an inner journey, where the act of travelling through this unstable landscape may attain an inner goal, more important than the apparent destination.

Something extraordinary happens when the protagonists reach the threshold of their destination, the Room, in *Stalker*. Having argued and fought, they do not go in – they stop.

MAKING

The camera then quietly lifts and glides away from them, over the threshold and into the Room. It transpires that, having accompanied the three men on their journey, we, the film's viewers, are being taken into the Room. Perhaps Tarkovsky is confronting us with a challenge: what is *our* deepest wish?

Accepting that challenge by designing and building one's own house is also in some way a spiritual quest, a journey to a real 'Room' where one's deepest wishes might be granted. In his book *Perfect in Weakness: Faith in Tarkovsky's Stalker* (2019), Colin Heber-Percy discusses the symbiotic

NITHURST SEEN FROM THE EAST

HANS VREDEMAN DE VRIES, PERSPECTIVE, PART 1: PLATE 10, *LEIDEN*, 1604–5

relationship between fantasy and reality in cinema – that each helps to define the other – and says: 'If the border between fantasy and reality were to be too clearly demarcated and policed ... this essential element of confusion, of failure to understand, to grasp, would be lost, and we would mistakenly take ourselves to be sure of where we stood. It is the job of science fiction, of fantasy, of tragic theatre to show that where we stand may not be where we think we stand, that struggle and fallibility is part and parcel of the process.'[8]

Heber-Percy seems to be saying that the film's power lies in the way it makes us question our assumptions, and like all great art, *Stalker* asks questions to which we struggle to find answers. In discussing the perimeter of the Zone, he says: 'The very pointlessness of the border, its arbitrary nature, causes us to rethink or call into question the neat tidy schema we have learned to bring with us into the cinema. Our expectations and preconceptions relating to genre, narrative, plotting and character are all destabilized by the experience of Stalker.'[9]

Can architecture engage with 'this essential element of confusion'? How might the making of a house subvert our expectations in a way that brings meaning to everyday situations? How might it draw the quotidian and the cosmic into fruitful reciprocity? Nithurst's design combines the 'theatre of life' with aspects of dreams and poetic associations, making use of paradox and anachronism, with stratagems aimed at 'destabilising' our expectations of what a building, a house, might be.

Seen from the east, Nithurst appears as a geometric abstraction of the hill visible in the distance in Hilliard's painting. Drawing on the Renaissance perspective studies of Hans Vredeman de Vries and on Robert Mangold's 1970s Minimalist artworks, this brick house rises in three steps through three storeys – a tower and not a tower, a hill and not a hill. The house's form gives it a sense of movement towards the south, and blurs of darker bricks streaming behind the arched 'Diocletian' windows reinforce a sense of 'bounce' and movement. The paradoxical nature of this contrast between what is clearly a heavy, immobile masonry building and a sense of movement, is combined with a game-of-scale, introduced by the use of extra-wide mortar joints between the bricks. An impression of a modern house wrapped in a Roman ruin is created, so following the approach track around the house we encounter paradox, contradiction and anachronism through the way that materials, forms and building technologies have been brought together.

This destabilisation, which began on the outside at Nithurst, continues when we go inside. Clearly the way that dreams, memories and associations are brought to bear on the design of the spaces has links to Surrealism. The architectural writer and teacher Dalibor Vesely spoke of the hidden, or 'latent' cultural associations belonging to typical 'situations', for example eating, working, and so on, and wrote about the way that the Surrealists invoked the 'oneiric house' as a paradigm of creativity in the service of their goal of reconciling the world of dreams with that of reality. Vesely described how Surrealism's 'main characteristics are the introverted nature of experience, immanent representation of transcendental phenomena and the intimate nature of the space in which the world of the Surrealists is situated. The space itself can be visualised as a private domain of a house.'[10]

At Nithurst the main space has echoes of a medieval great hall, of a town square, castle walls, of a chapel – and of a key scene in Tarkovsky's film. It carries personal memories of buildings in England, in Venice and the Veneto, and of images of industrial structures. The juxtaposition of these layered associations with the activities of everyday life lends a potency and an emotional dimension to those situations: cooking, drawing, making, talking, eating, children doing their homework, and so on.

Vesely discussed the way that the move towards introversion and the location of culture in the house began in the sixteenth century: 'This took place in the formation of the late Renaissance villa, an idealised substitute for the existing urban culture ... The first signs of the transformation were expressed already in the Renaissance, saying that the house is a small city and the city a large house ... In a later development, the museum entered the private dwelling where museum rooms and objects were intertwined with objects and spaces of everyday life. A very good example is Sir John Soane's Museum in London.'[11]

In this book, Corinna Dean observes that the artefacts and artworks at Nithurst can be seen as fragments of a wider culture, and that these objects subtly illuminate and represent the thematic ordering of the house. Some objects have clear meanings, others work at a subconscious level, and they have affinities with the notion of the Memory Theatre. Like the artefacts and objects glimpsed underwater in Tarkovsky's scene where the Stalker sleeps, these cultural fragments point the way on the journey through the house. The chosen objects also have an affective emphasis towards engaging our emotions. This idea of a 'journey' within the house is further explored through a game played with ideas of perspective, and through the materials of its making.

SENSE

Discussing the cinema of Tarkovsky, the architect and writer Juhani Pallasmaa says that the director's images of rooms 'with rain pouring through the roof ... are among the most fascinating architectural images ever created. Although they are scenes of erosion, they radiate a spectacular

HANS VREDEMAN DE VRIES, PERSPECTIVE, PART 1: PLATE 29, *LEIDEN*, 1604–5

Orizon   *A*   *B*

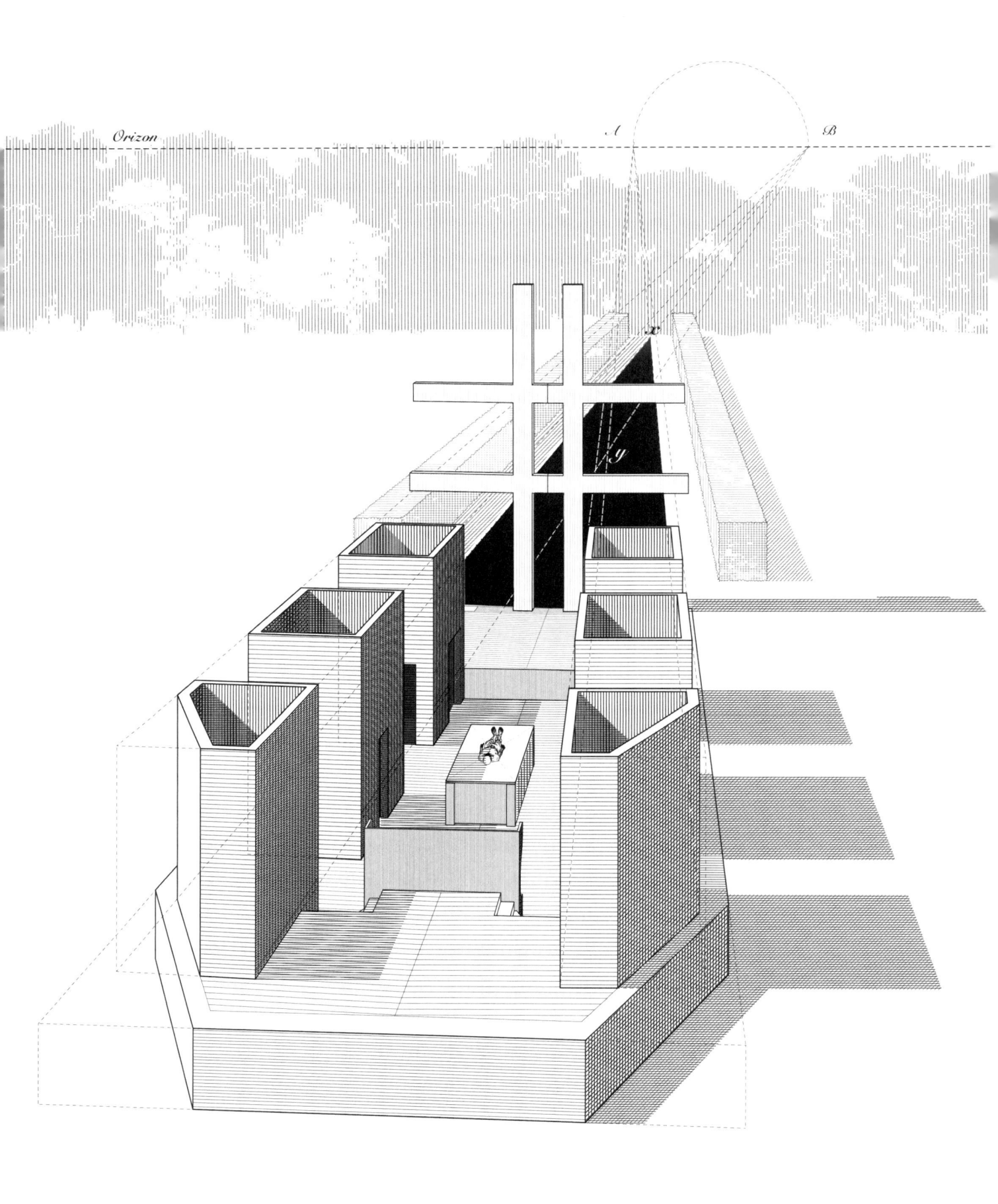

beauty and purity of feeling. They possess an almost sacred or ecclesiastical presence. These spaces cannot protect the human body, but they can house its soul. The wealth of details, images, and associations, and the fusion of figure and ground, matter and light in these images bring to mind the complexity of space, ornament, painted illusion and light in the interiors of Bavarian rococo churches.'[12]

The intense sensory experience of entering the house through the narrow, dark, log-filled entrance hall has been touched on in this book's other essays. 'From here, we arrive in a corner of the large main space, with views across the room and out through a high window, up to the trees of Henry Percy's distant hilltop. This oblique entry gives a sense of having joined a space with its own much bigger – and slightly disconcerting – ordering principle. Converging at three degrees from parallel, the six concrete towers and outer walls here create a false perspective as we look along the space, making it feel particularly long and large. It is the start of a pair of journeys through the house: one horizontal, the other vertical.

In his essay *Perspective as Symbolic Form* (1927), the art historian Erwin Panofsky criticised the way in which western culture since the Renaissance had identified perspective with truth and with mathematical precision. Panofsky and others who followed have seen that perspective is a construction that creates images that are similar to how we see the world, but not a truthful, exact description of it. Not only is the development of perspective now seen as having created a way of seeing the world, but also the method by which perspective is constructed can be considered to have influenced how buildings are designed and how we understand space. We can easily assume perspective is what the world is, and therefore start to 'read' space based on assumptions about orthogonal space and how it is constructed.

At Nithurst, because the walls are not parallel, but converge, we perceive the space as longer when seen from one end, and wider when seen from the other. The angle by which the walls vary from being parallel is so slight as to be barely noticeable: the converging walls take the idea of perspective as a 'symbolic form', and deliberately play with it, thereby undermining our assumptions about the space. By doing so it becomes possible to turn the idea of perspective to other ends.

The converging walls create a different relationship with the idea of the vanishing point. Instead of encapsulating a mathematical idea of infinity in relation to our eye (as in 'proper' perspective constructions), it can be identified as a specific point or vertical line in space in relation to the house – thereby generating an idea of finitude that could, perhaps, be seen as analogous to the finite nature of our own lives in the world.

It has been observed that Renaissance perspective, with its parallel structures and gridded spaces receding into the distance, carries the implication of an idea of movement. At Nithurst, this implied movement is exaggerated by the false perspective, and is mapped onto the idea of the journey to a destination – a destination to be reached by moving through this large space.

This destination – our version of Tarkovsky's Room – is reached after leaving the main space and passing through a dark, constrained passage. Again, we enter obliquely. In *Stalker*, the destination is a strange, derelict industrial space where water 'rains' from the ceiling and flows across the floor. As mentioned previously, this moment of apotheosis in the film could be seen as a challenge to the viewer: 'you are in the Room: what now?' At Nithurst, our 'Room' is a family sitting room – but it can be used and understood in different ways. It is a comfortable space for relaxing, but it is presided over by objects that recapitulate some of the issues of anachronism, contradiction and dystopia that we have already encountered. Tapestries, abstract art, religious sculptures and scientific images combine with stained concrete and long views into nature. On one level, it is simply a beautiful room, but other clues are present. For example, the fireplace sits centrally in the symmetrical space, facing due south through tall windows towards the midday sun. This dialogue draws the eye out into the landscape.

The sitting room's relationship with the long south garden is central to the idea of a journey embodied in the house. The garden is flanked by converging hedges, which had existed for at least 150 years, and the strange way that these hedges create a false perspective informed how the house's design engages with its site. Whilst the sitting room at Nithurst appears to be the destination (a room in which our deepest wishes might be granted), it also focuses attention on the long south garden. The recurring human dream of a return to a prelapsarian state is frequently identified with gardens. At Nithurst, the multiple 'vanishing points' of the house's converging walls all meet within this garden, paradoxically implying that the garden contains the limits of the world.

This room's windows also reveal the garden's brooding backdrop of woodland, the west window emphasising the beauty and mystery of these woods, silhouetted nightly as the sun goes down behind them: a prefiguring of death and the hoped-for revelation of meaning that might accompany life's end. Whilst the west window looks through an outer brick arch, the view from the south windows is through a grid of columns. This grid rises up the south facade, presiding over the south garden. This vertical aspect introduces the second of the journeys through the house

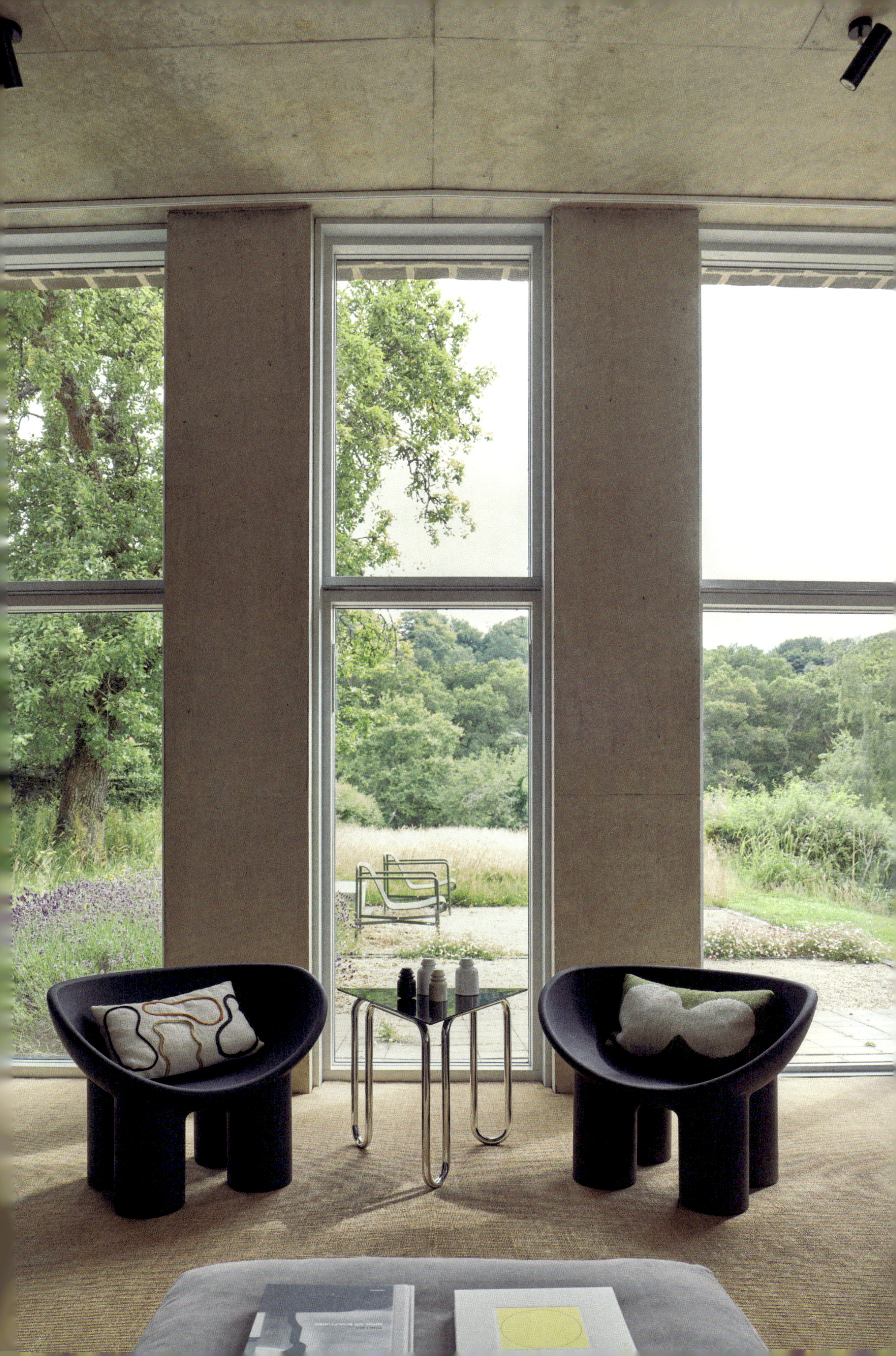

JACKET HAWKER SIDDELEY
LOCALITY BEDFORDSHIRE
DATE 28.5.13
J. Eddon

that began in the main space. The route is via a serpentine staircase and leads to a pair of full-height doors on the first-floor landing, beyond which is the final tapering staircase to the top floor. At the top of this stair is a kind of glazed loggia: a platform looking out over the long south garden, with its implied vanishing points. We are standing on the top level of the facade grid, perched as if one of the birdlike spirit forms in Paul Nash's *Mansions of the Dead*.

Perhaps, like Henry Percy, or the Stalker, we all hope, or fear, that a hidden geometry is at work in our lives. The buildings we create for ourselves can frame and mediate the relationship between the quotidian and the cosmic, between how we engage with the world through our senses and how we seek a spiritual dimension in our hearts. Architecture can be an ordering device for setting these moving parts in motion in relation to each other; but if a work of architecture is also to be a work of art, it should plot a route between certainty and doubt, it should ask questions rather than giving answers, and perhaps project or imagine a place beyond itself – a vanishing point that we can't see but perhaps can sense.

1. Juhani Pallasmaa, *The Architecture of Image: Existential Space in Cinema*, Rakennustieto Publishing, Helsinki, 2001, p.92.
2. I am indebted to Patrick Lynch for this subtitle. After visiting Nithurst he noted our copy of the Talking Heads album *Stop Making Sense*, and identified this with the house's thematics.
3. Peter Jerome, *Petworth. From the Beginnings to 1660*, The Window Press, 2002. The history of Petworth 'yields no figure more heroic, more mysterious, and ultimately more tragic than James, a rural Prometheus who fought Henry Percy to a standstill...', p.96.
4. Henry Percy, the 9th Earl of Northumberland (1564–1632), was a well-known Elizabethan intellectual and cultural figure. He was known as the 'Wizard Earl' because of his scientific and alchemical experiments and his large library.
5. An *impresa* is a portrait in which the likeness is accompanied by a combination of symbolic images and mottos, which are intended to convey a personal message about the sitter. These were pioneered by Nicholas Hilliard, drawing on Italian Renaissance ideas, and appealed to the Elizabethans' love of 'devices'. I am grateful to Richard Dollamore for bringing this image to my attention.
6. Henry Percy used a telescope to make a map of the moon around the same time as Galileo.
7. Henry Percy is thought to have been part of a proto-scientific circle that included John Dee, interested in the hermetic aspects of alchemy as a spiritual quest, where the gold of the 'Philosopher's Stone' is seen as a metaphor for attaining a state of spiritual enlightenment. In the twentieth century Carl Jung explored these ideas in the context of psychoanalysis (C.G. Jung, *Psychology and Alchemy*, Routledge, London, 1944).
8. Colin Heber-Percy, *Perfect in Weakness: Faith in Tarkovsky's Stalker*, Cascade Books, 2019, p.58.
9. ibid., p.60.
10. Dalibor Vesely, *The Latent World of Architecture. Selected Essays*, Alexandra Stara and Peter Carl, eds, 2023, p.220.
11. ibid., p.220.
12. Pallasmaa, *The Architecture of Image*, 2001, p.91.

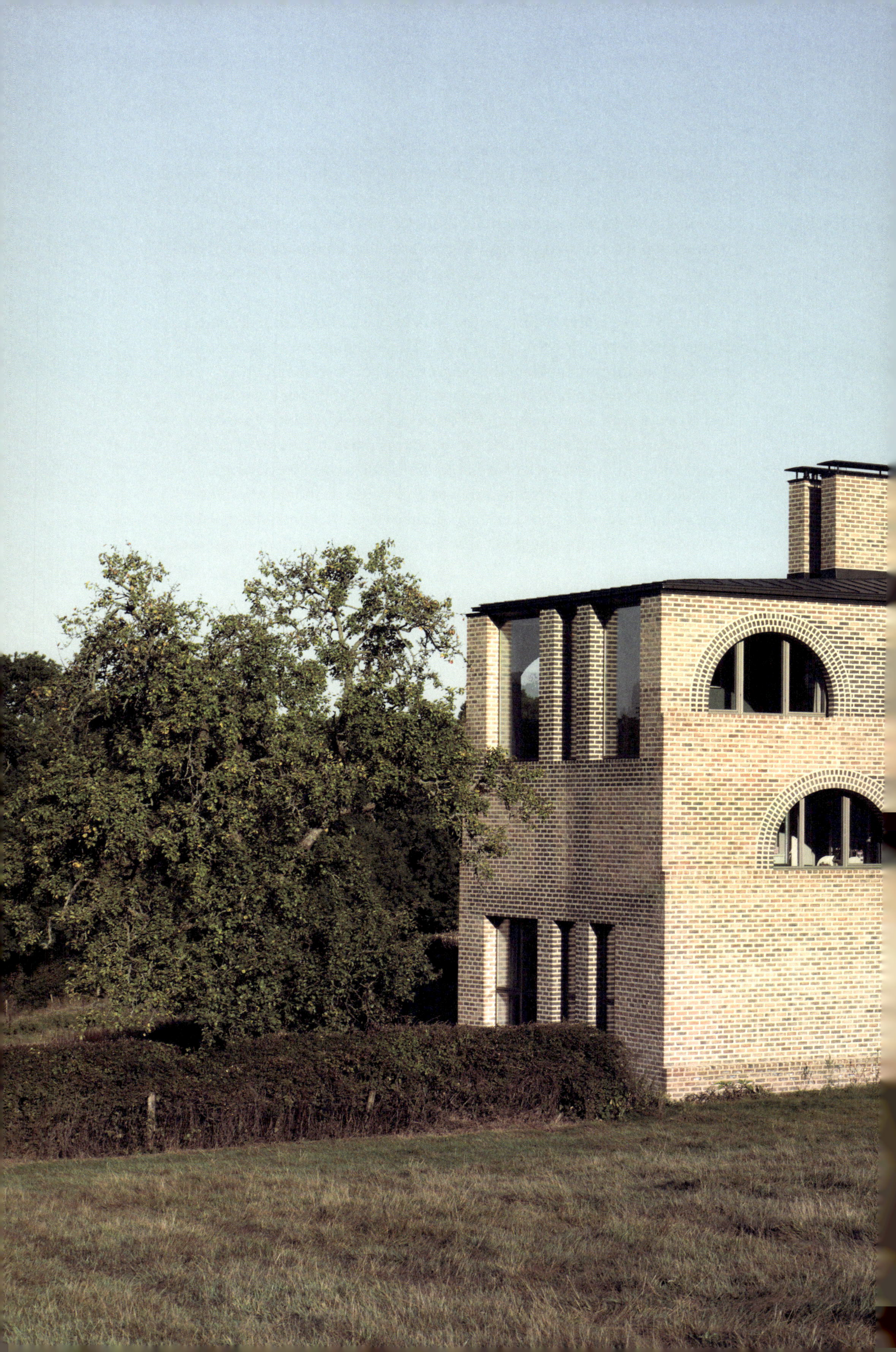

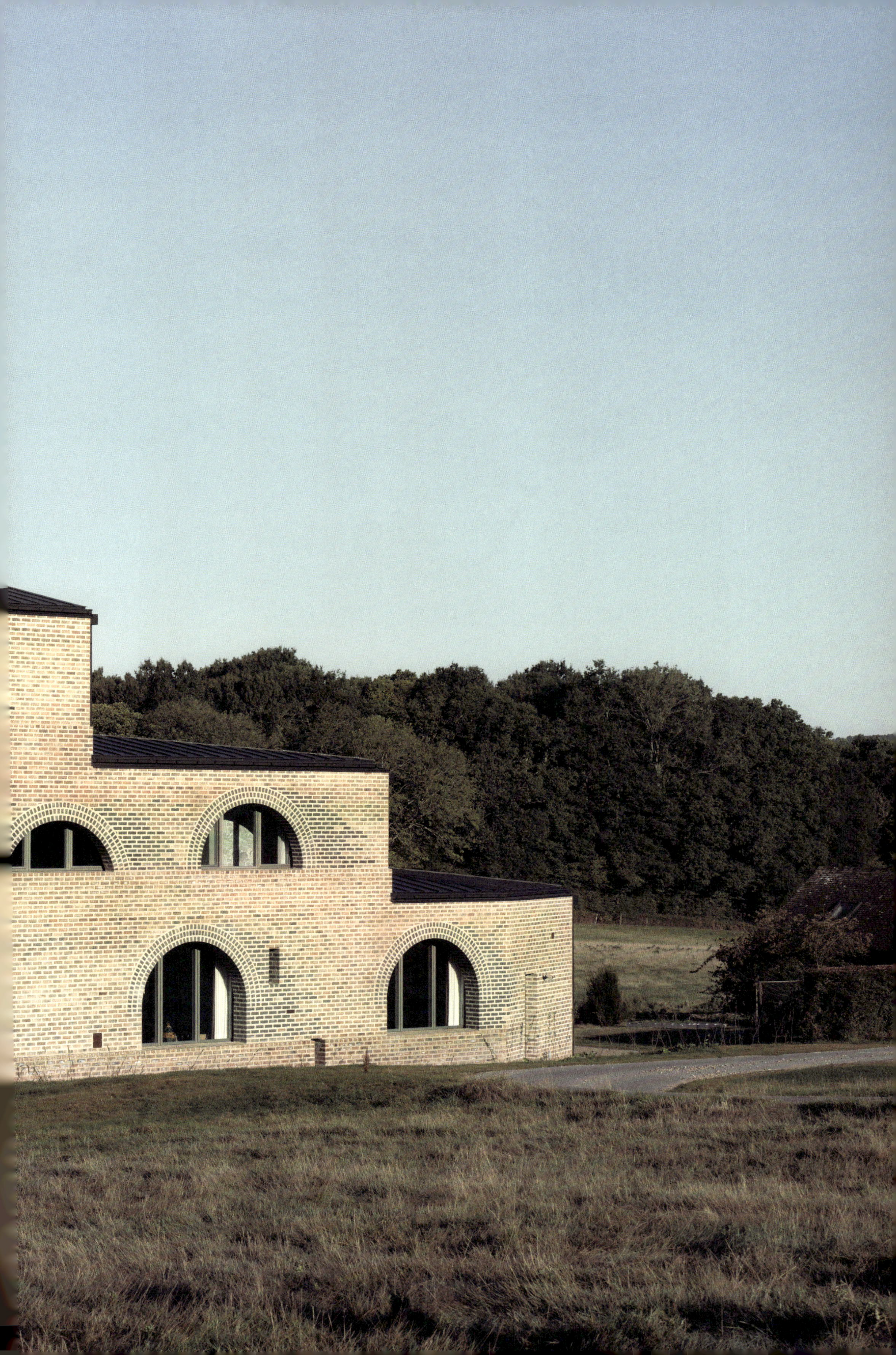

Here we are...home, at last

POINTS OF REFERENCE – V

TAKERO SHIMAZAKI: Nithurst represents a compelling story of the architect's journey and his inspirations – a 'zone' where 'your deepest wishes will come true'. During my visit I found myself questioning whether so many layers and references were really needed to make a good piece of architecture. Because this is quite simply a very beautiful house.

Yet, having watched *Stalker* again, and contemplating why we are drawn to build, I came to better understand this house, and see how it is absolutely necessary that these stories are embedded within its walls. It is a building etched with rich tales of architecture and the family. And even though the house is very much engaged with the present and the specific context of its site, it belongs to the long and continuous history of marking the land with a building. Richards describes the house as a modern Roman ruin, an impression maintained in the more 'industrial' interior by the way the outer brick skin can be read through openings in the concrete 'body'.

Like Palladio's villas, Nithurst is a singular artefact that embodies the idea of the city and the collective memory. The labyrinthine qualities of the connecting routes, the vast main room and the surrounding smaller, more intimate, spaces all give a sense of the city within the house. The main room is both a public plaza and a basilica, and the first-floor landing is a mini piazza. Nithurst is a monolithic, monumental sculpture in the tradition of country villas, but one where the allusions to urban, civic life fuse with rural qualities of space, landscape and air.

ANDREI TARKOVSKY, STILL FROM *STALKER*, 1979

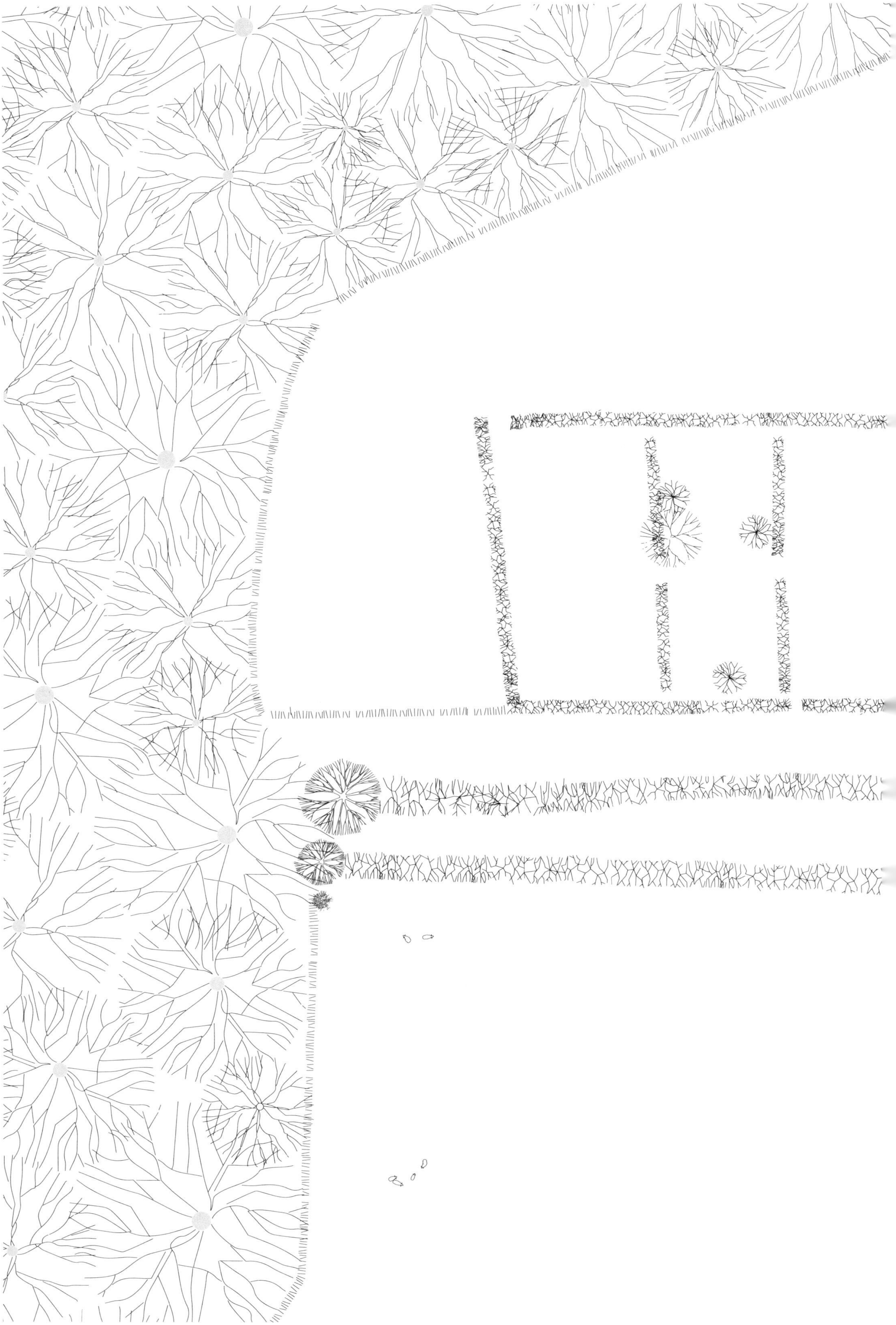

0   5   20   50 M

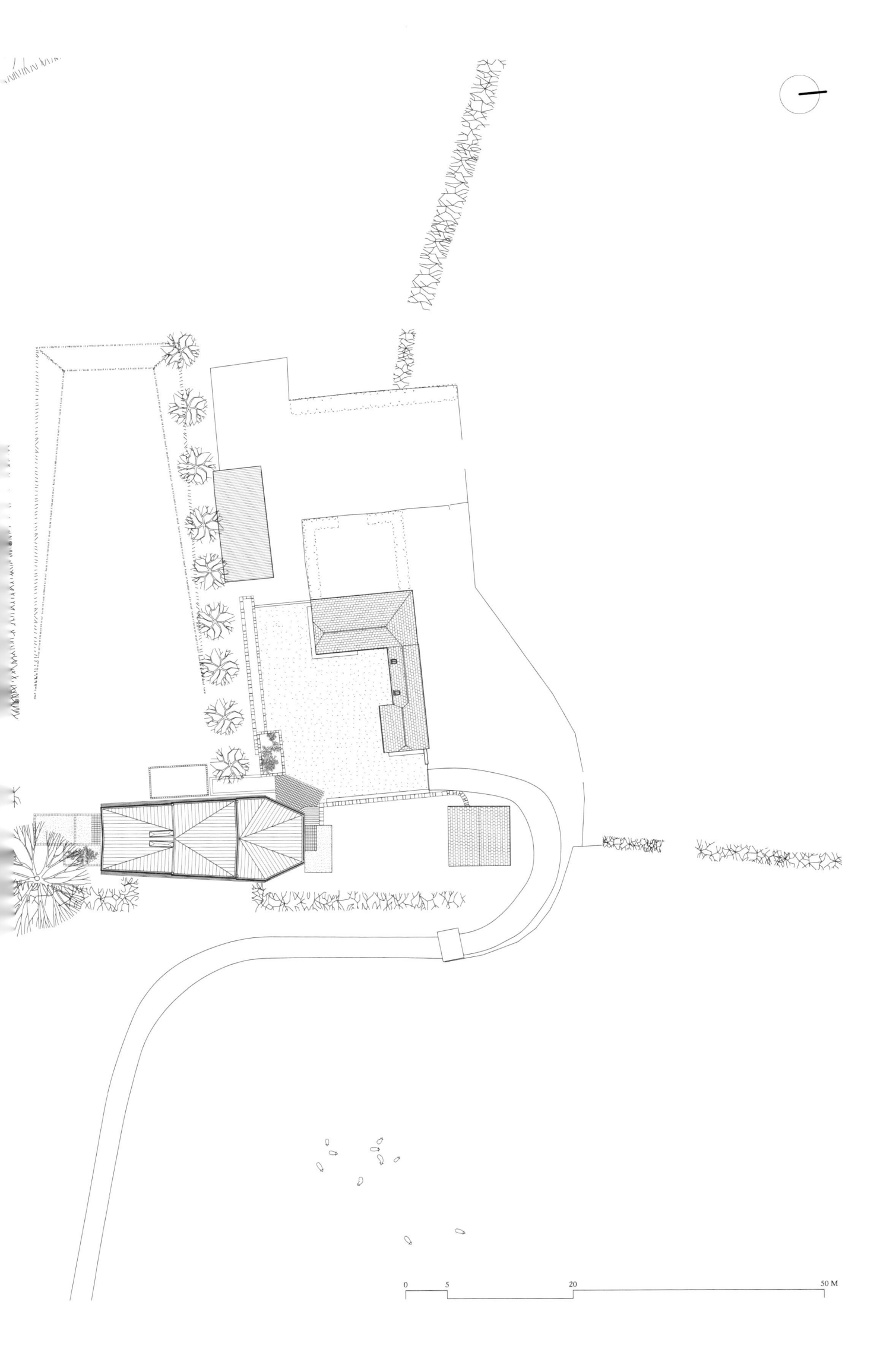

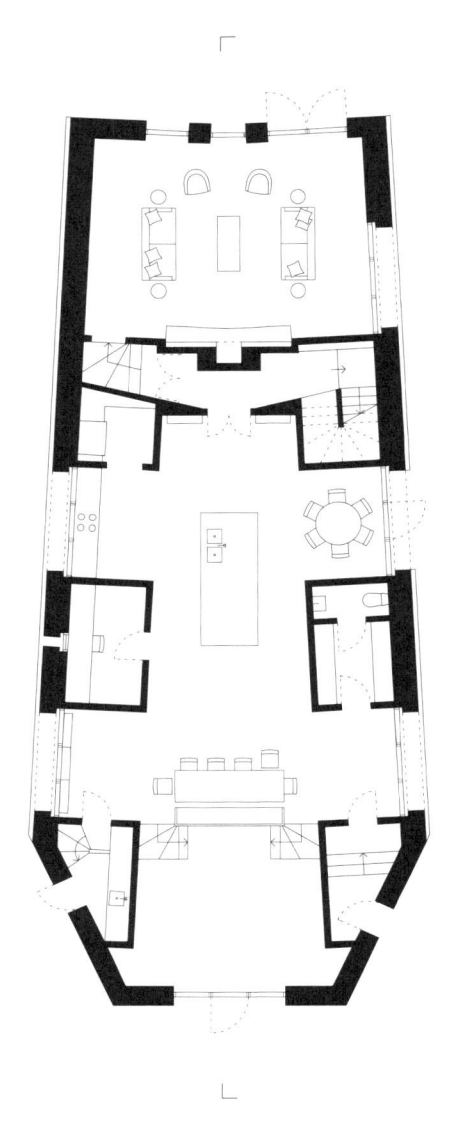

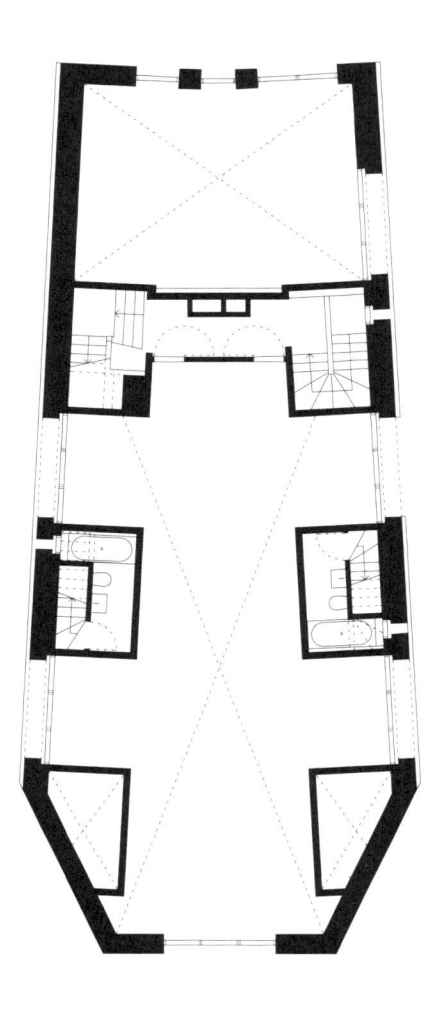

0   5   10 M

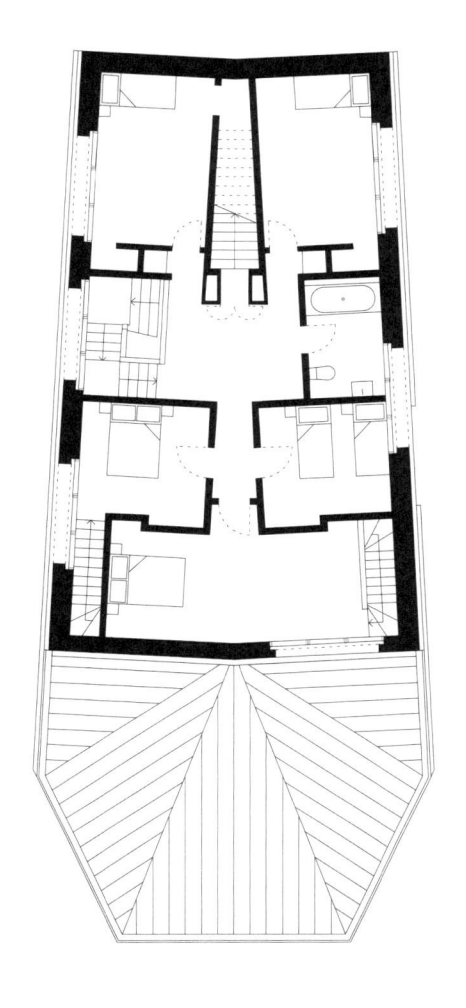

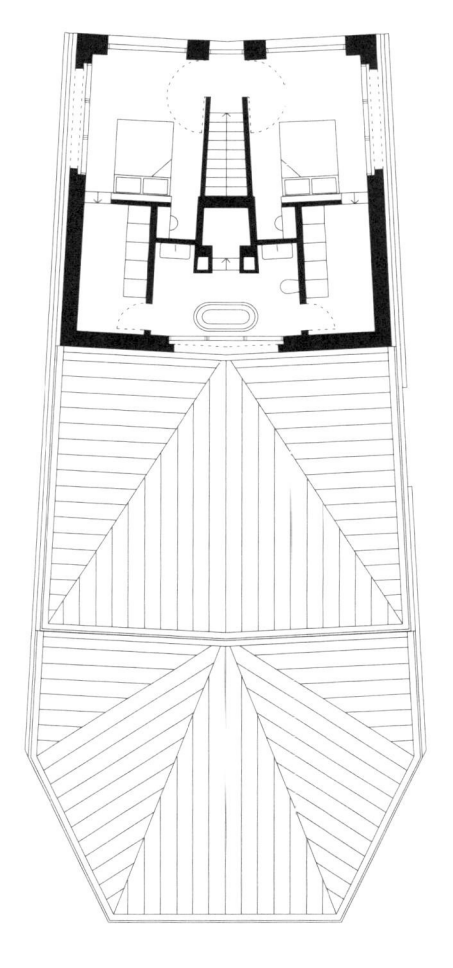

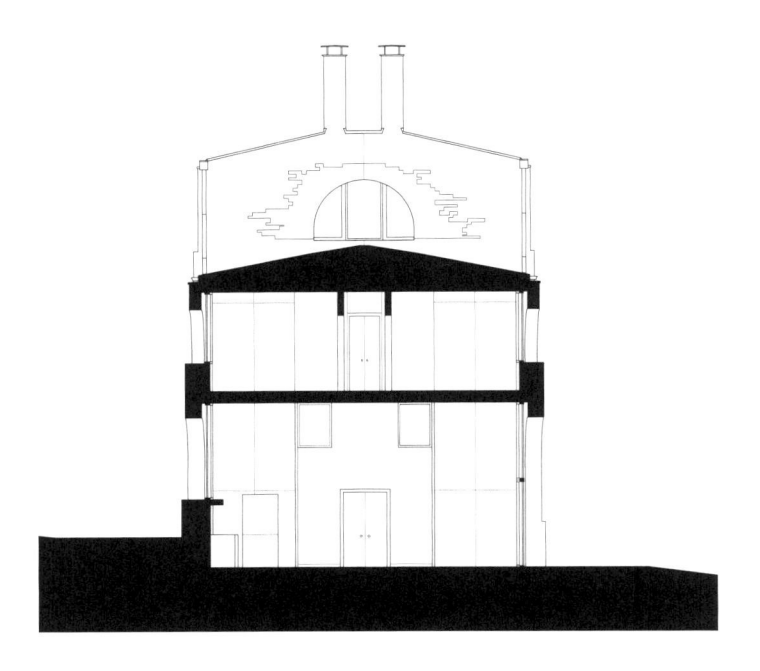

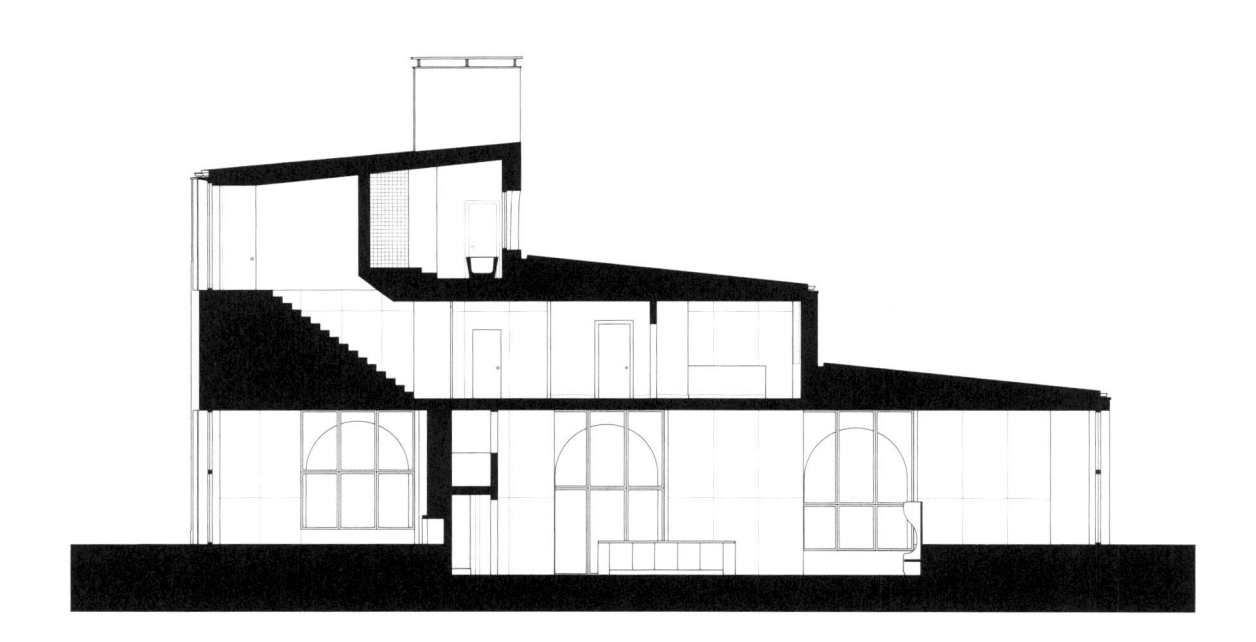

0 5 10 M

ACKNOWLEDGEMENTS

A book and a building both depend for their realisation on the work of a wide team of people, and the commitment and determination to drive the project through to completion. *Here We Are, Home At Last* would not have been possible without the commitment and determination of Claire Curtice, who also demonstrated great patience in shepherding its production over a period of years. Rosa Nussbaum's graphic design shows her deep understanding of the book's texts, and also of the house and its contents. Thanks are also due to Val Rose and all at Lund Humphries, to the writers whose work appears in the book, to Susannah Stone for sourcing imagery and to Tasnim Eshraqi for his work on the drawings.

Special thanks must go to photographers Tim Brotherton and Katie Lock, for their photographs of Nithurst, and for their friendship over many years.

Many collaborators at Adam Richards Architects contributed to the process of completing Nithurst, with particular thanks to Sam Dawkins, Joe Mackey, Giles Hampton and David Rozwadowski. Thanks also to structural engineers Structure Workshop, services engineers p3r, quantity surveyor Mark Price and planning consultants Whaleback.

The house was ably built by Matthew Duke of Garsden Pepper and his staff and subcontractors, and by SMD Formwork. Thanks are also due to the artists whose work appears in the house, especially HelenA Pritchard, and to Richard Dollamore and Graham Morrison for their support during the planning process.

Finally, I would like to thank my family – Jessica, Esme, Eddie and Ivan – who tolerated many freezing cold hours up ladders, and who continue to tolerate me.

And Percy the dog.

CONTRIBUTORS

TAKERO SHIMAZAKI is an architect and a director of Takero Shimazaki Architects/t-sa, London, UK. He studied at University of Wales, Cardiff and The Bartlett, UCL. He has worked for Richard Rogers Partnership, Itsuko Hasegawa, and Alison and Peter Smithson. Completed projects by t-sa include OSh House, Centre for Sight, Leicester Print Workshop, Royal Academy of Dance and two cinemas (Bloomsbury and Camden) for Curzon. Takero is also a Diploma Unit Tutor at London Metropolitan University.

JEREMY MUSSON is the author of many books on the English country house and related subjects. He has worked for the Victorian Society and then the National Trust. He was an architectural writer and editor for *Country Life* magazine. Since late 2007, he has been an independent author and heritage consultant. He was also presenter and co-writer of the two BBC Two series of *The Curious House Guest*. A Fellow of the Society of Antiquaries, he also teaches for the University of Cambridge and New York University (London programmes) and is a trustee of the Historic Houses Foundation.

GEOFF DYER is the author of four novels and numerous non-fiction books, including *Zona* about Andrei Tarkovsky's film *Stalker*. He has won many literary awards and his books have been translated into 24 languages.

CORINNA DEAN is a senior lecturer at the University of Westminster and a member of the Emerging Territories research group where she explores issues around urban ecologies. Her work ranges from founding ARCA, the Archive for Rural Contemporary Architecture, to working with regenerative materials to engage broad communities, social and ecological.

ADAM RICHARDS is a British architect whose work has encompassed architecture, interior design and furniture. As well as designing private houses, his practice has earned a reputation for making highly crafted buildings for the arts, cultural and heritage sectors, including Ditchling Museum of Art + Craft in Sussex. He has taught architecture at Cambridge University and Kingston University.

TIM BROTHERTON and KATIE LOCK are the photographic duo Brotherton–Lock who specialise in high quality architectural and interior photography. Working in partnership, they use their artistic and architectural backgrounds to expertly capture visuals that convey the unique experiences of the spaces and places they photograph. On site they work as a team using digital large-format technologies and digital SLRs.

IMAGE CREDITS

Numbers refer to pages. All plans and drawings © Adam Richards Architects unless otherwise stated.

© Artothek: 35
Photographs © Brotherton–Lock: 1, 2–3, 4–5, 10–11, 12, 14, (work Robert Mangold © ARS, NY and DACS, London 2024), 15, 16–17, 18, 20–21, 23, 24, 27, 28–29, 32, 33, 48–49 (work © Keith Wilson), 50 (work © unknown), 51, 52–53 and 54–55 (work Robert Mangold © ARS, NY and DACS, London 2024), 56 (work © HelenA Pritchard), 57 (work © unknown), 58–59, 60, 61, 62–63, 64, 66–67 (work © Simon Norfolk), 68 (work © HelenA Pritchard), 69 (artist unknown), 70–71 (work © Simon Norfolk), 78 (artist unknown), 79 (artist unknown), 80 (work © Le Corbusier © F.L.C. / ADAGP, Paris and DACS, London 2024), 80 (artist unknown), 81 (artist unknown), 82–83 (work © Claire Pestaille), 90 (artist unknown), 91 (artist unknown), 93, 94 (artist unknown), 95 (work © The Elisabeth Frink Estate and Archive. All Rights Reserved, DACS 2024), 96–97, 98–99 (work © Bruce McLean. All Rights Reserved, DACS 2024), 102–103, 105, 106, 109, 113, 121, 122 (work © Jane Edden), 124–125, 136–137, 138–139, 140
© Digital image Rijksmuseum Amsterdam Nicholas Hilliard: 7, 110
© Mosfilm/Chetvyortoe Tvorchesko/Diltz/Bridgeman: 26
© Digital photo: Tate Images: 109
© HelenA Pritchard: 30–31
© Adam Richards: 73, 100
© Mosfilm/Chetvyortoe Tvorchesko/Diltz/: 126
© Hans Vredeman de Vries: 8, 114, 117

First published in 2024 by Lund Humphries

Lund Humphries
Huckletree Shoreditch
Alphabeta Building
18 Finsbury Square
London EC2A 1AH
UK
www.lundhumphries.com

Here We Are, Home At Last: The Architecture of Nithurst
© Adam Richards, 2024
'Points of Reference' by Takero Shimazaki first published in *Architecture Today*, November 2019 © Takero Shimazaki, 2024
'Conversations with the Past' © Jeremy Musson, 2024
'Zone Dogs' © Geoff Dyer, 2024
'A Repository for Fragments' © Corinna Dean, 2024
'Vanishing Point' © Adam Richards, 2024
All rights reserved

ISBN: 978-1-84822-700-2

A Cataloguing-in-Publication record for this book is available from the British Library

All rights reserved. No part of this publication may be reproduced, stored in a retrieval system or transmitted in any form or by any means, electrical, mechanical or otherwise, without first seeking the permission of the copyright owners and publishers. Every effort has been made to seek permission to reproduce the images in this book. Any omissions are entirely unintentional, and details should be addressed to the publishers.

Adam Richards has asserted his right under the Copyright, Designs and Patents Act, 1988, to be identified as the Author of this Work.

Designed by Studio Christopher Victor
Set in King's Caslon and Fakt
Printed in Italy

Front cover: © Adam Richards Architects
Back cover: Nithurst, east elevation © Brotherton–Lock

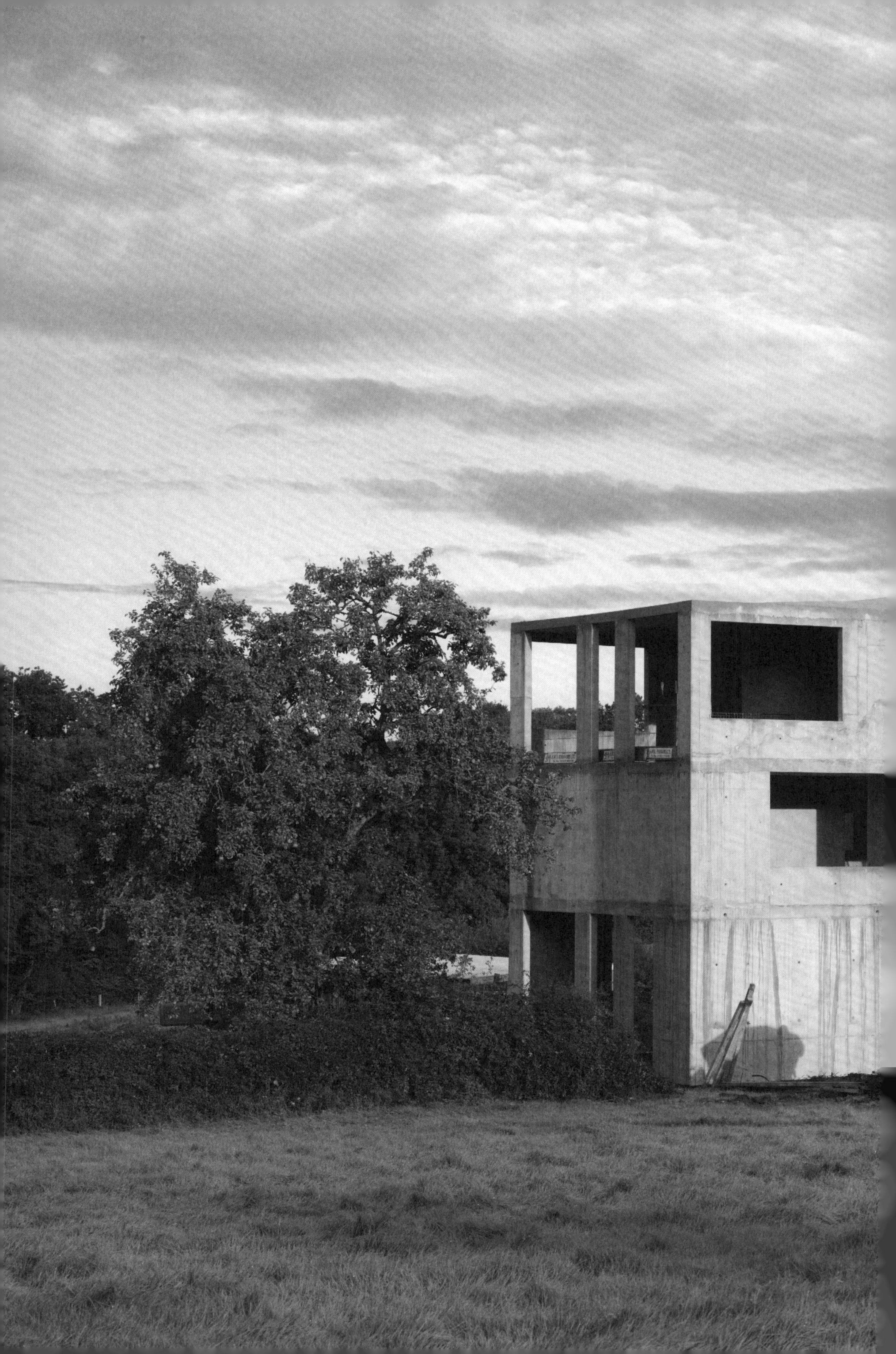